Legal Guide to Microenterprise Development

Susan R. Jones

ABA Section of
BUSINESS LAW
Practical Resources for the Business Lawyer

ABA
Defending Liberty
Pursuing Justice

Printed in the United States of America.

Library of Congress Cataloging-in-Publication Data

Jones, Susan R., 1957–
Legal guide to microenterprise development / by Susan Jones.— 1st ed.
p. cm.
Includes bibliographical references.
ISBN 1-59031-295-3 (pbk.)
1. Small business—Law and legislation—United States. I. Title.

KF1659.J66 2004
346.73′0652—dc22 2004017375

Discounts are available for books ordered in bulk. Special consideration is given to state and local bars, CLE programs, and other bar-related organizations. Inquire at ABA Publishing, American Bar Association, 321 North Clark Street, Chicago, Illinois 60610.

08 07 06 05 04 5 4 3 2 1

Contents

Acknowledgments

The microenterprise development industry has grown substantially since 1998 when the first edition of this book was published. Legal and public policy support for MED has also grown. A rise in business law pro bono services heightened the prospect that non-profit microenterprise development programs may have access to general legal services for myriad legal issues including loan document preparation, while microbusinesses may benefit from start up legal assistance in corporate tax, and intellectual property law.

This book would not have been possible without the support of the ABA Commission on Homelessness & Poverty, ABA Publishing and the Association for Enterprise Opportunity. I am especially grateful to Amy Horton Newell, Myles Lynk, Jackie McGlamery, Suzy Bibko, Susan Douglas Taylor, Joan Meier, Bill Edwards, Mark Greenberg, and the community of MED practitioners. I would also like to thank Mary Graeter, Selim Ablo, Sarah Hensley, and Kyle Waldner for their excellent research assistance. Readers and contributors to the first edition included Patricia Hanrahan, Legal Services Corporation, formerly Staff Director of the ABA Commission on Homelessness and Poverty; Peter Manzo and Andrea Ball, formerly of Public Counsel; Sojeila Silva, Executive Director of Seed Capital Development Fund, Ltd.; Mari Riddle, former Executive Director of the Coalition for Women's Economic Development; Prof. Peter Pitegoff, University at Buffalo Law School; Prof. Alberto Benitez, The George Washington University Law School; Prof. Louis Solomon, The George Washington University Law School; Mark Greenberg, Director of Policy, Center for Law and Social Policy; Melissa Bradley, Community Affairs Specialist, Office of Thrift Supervision, Department of Treasury; Kathryn E. Walsh, formerly an ABA legal intern now at King & Spalding, LLP; Kevin Stein, Staff Attorney, East Palo Alto Law Project; and the 1994 Commission on Homelessness and Poverty Members: David Dedyo, Suzanne Gladstone, David Kirkpatrick, Joseph Solee, and Diane Dorius. I would also like to extend my appreciation to my colleagues at the George Washington University Law School who have supported by work in many ways.

I would also like to thank my husband, G.H. Abasi Johnson, and my parents, Dr. Shirley Jones and Mr. Sande R. Jones, Sr., and my brother, Sande R. Jones, Jr., for their love and support.

Susan R. Jones
Professor of Clinical Law
The George Washington University Law School
Director, Small Business Clinic/Community
Economic Development Project

Foreword

Microenterprise development is a community economic development and anti-poverty strategy designed to create jobs through self-employment. By turning interests, hobbies, and skills into small businesses, microentrepreneurs, many of them women, minorities, and members of underserved communities, fulfill their dreams of running a small business. Microenterprise development organizations provide financial, technical, social, and business support to individual entrepreneurs, most of whom lack business experience. Although these potential entrepreneurs possess the drive, creativity, and talents to create and market a product needed in their communities, the resources required to initiate and sustain small businesses are often beyond their reach because they lack credit histories or good credit, assets, family role models, mentors, and formal or business education.

As with any business, creating and maintaining the entity, no matter how small, involves legal issues and responsibilities including tax, regulatory, licensing, contracts, and liability matters. Pro bono attorneys who are willing to help these microentrepreneurs, or the organizations that sponsor them, will make a critical difference. This book is written to inspire and guide lawyers who have volunteered to represent microentrepreneurs and their businesses, as well as the microenterprise development organizations that facilitate the development of these small businesses.

Generally, practitioners of corporate, banking, and tax law spend much of their time counseling large industries. While some of the principles and legal parameters are the same in microenterprises as in larger businesses, other elements are quite different. Keeping these differences in mind, this book seeks to offer an overview of issues affecting microenterprise programs and resources in the industry, as well as provide guidance for microentrepreneurs and those who assist them.

Chapters 1 and 2 introduce the legal community to the burgeoning microenterprise development industry and the lawyer's role in helping microenterprise programs. Chapters 3 and 4 discuss legal formation issues for new or expanding microenterprises and program planning issues. Chapters 5 and 6 review funding, legal and business issues for microenterprises and microenterprise development programs, and Chapter 7 is a summary of future trends in the industry. The appendix provides legal resources for attorneys representing microenterprise programs and their clients—the microenterprises.

CHAPTER **1**

Introduction

A. Microenterprise Development and Its History

Microenterprise development (MED) is an economic development strategy that provides small loans, business training, and technical assistance to people starting very small businesses. The concept of microenterprise development originated in the 1970s in Latin America, Asia, Africa, and other parts of the developing world as a strategy to alleviate poverty.[1] One of the most successful and renowned microenterprise programs is the Grameen Bank in Bangladesh.[2]

During the 1970s in the United States, efforts to channel money and assets to low-income neighborhoods focused on affordable housing de-

1. Two famous examples are Banco Sol in La Paz, Bolivia, and Caja Labral Popular in Mondragon, Spain. Others credit the women's movement as an influential catalyst.

2. See Alex Counts, *Give Us Credit* (1996); Muhammad Yunus et al., Banker to the Poor: Micro-Lending and the Battle Against World Poverty (PublicAffairs 2003); David Bornstein, The Price of a Dream: The Story of the Grameen Bank and the Idea That Is Helping the Poor to Change Their Lives (Simon & Schuster 1999).

While a discussion of international microenterprise issues is outside the scope of this book, it is noteworthy that support for microenterprise development has been an important part of U.S. foreign assistance for the past three decades. The Microenterprise for Self Reliance and International Anti-Corruption Act of 2000 (*Microenterprise for Self-Reliance and International Anti-Corruption Act of 2000*), Pub. L. 106-309, 114 Stat. 1078 (2000)) authorizes grants by the U.S. Agency for International Development (USAID) to support poor entrepreneurs in foreign countries who typically live on less than one U.S. dollar a day. Emmy Simmons, *The Role of Microenterprise Assistance in U.S. Development Policy*, Feb. 5, 2004 *available at* mumbai.usconsulate.gov/wwwhwashnews1303.html, last visited June 18, 2004. *See also* Microenterprise Development in a Changing World, U.S. Agency for International Development Microenterprise Results Reporting for 2000, Dec. 2001 *available at* www.dec.org/pdf_docs/PDABW785.pdf (last visited June 27, 2004).

velopment and job training. Self-employment and entrepreneurial opportunities for low-income people were not emphasized. But microenterprise programs, some based on the famous Grameen Bank model, finally took root in the United States in the mid-1980s to serve low-income people and alleviate poverty.[3] Over time, however, microenterprise practitioners[4] became aware of a credit gap experienced by moderate-income persons, and others, such as women and minority entrepreneurs who often did not have access to commercial credit opportunities. To address this credit gap, the goals of microenterprise programs expanded from poverty alleviation to include job creation, broader community economic development in target areas, and human development.

Today, the term microenterprise development describes a wide range of programs which are custom-made for diverse settings; they also reflect varied purposes, values, and program designs. Over 750 microenterprise programs and supporting organizations now exist in all 50 states, the District of Columbia, the Mariana Islands, and Puerto Rico. In 2000, the majority of these programs assisted 99,945 individuals, of which 9,800 were borrowers.[5] Microenterprise development continues to grow; statewide and regional organizations complement the work of the Association for Enterprise Opportunity (AEO), the industry's trade association for the United States and Canada.[6]

Microenterprise models play an important role in state and national economic development agendas for job creation, community rebuild-

---

3. The first U.S. microenterprise program, Women Venture (formerly CHART/WEDCO) in St. Paul, Minnesota was started in 1983. See Self-Employment Learning Project, Aspen Institute, 1993 Microenterprise Briefing Packet: Facts and Figures on Seven U.S. Microenterprise Development Programs (1993) [hereinafter Packet].

4. In this book, the term practitioner refers to the staff of microenterprise programs and not to lawyers.

5. 2002 DIRECTORY OF U.S. MICROENTERPRISE PROGRAMS xv-xvi (Britton A. Walker & Amy Kays Blair eds., Microenterprise Fund for Innovation, Effectiveness, Learning and Dissemination (FIELD) 2002) [hereinafter 2002 Directory]; *see also* Robert Friedman & Puchka Sahay, *Six Steps Forward for Microenterprise Development*, The Entrepreneurial Economy Review, 1996 at 32 (estimating 750 microenterprise programs).

6. Founded in 1991, the Association for Enterprise Opportunity (AEO) is a national association of organizations committed to microenterprise development. Representing the U.S. microenterprise agenda, AEO's membership includes microenterprise practitioners, individuals, public agencies, funders, and others who share in its mission. AEO provides its members with a forum, information, and a voice to promote enterprise opportunity for people and communities with limited access to economic resources. For more information visit the Association for Enterprise Opportunity Website at www.microenterpriseworks.org. *See also* Stephanie N. Mehta, *Tiny Firms Find Growing Can be as Hard as Surviving: Microbusinesses Lack Providers of Funds, Advice to Expand to Next Level*, WALL ST. J., Mar. 25, 1997, at B2.

ing, and economic self-sufficiency. During the Clinton Administration, another manifestation of the microenterprise industry's national prominence was the Presidential Award for Excellence in Microenterprise Development. These non-monetary awards brought wider public attention to microenterprise development by recognizing programs that provide opportunities for people who lack access to traditional credit such as women, minorities, and low-income Americans. The Microcredit Summit, held on February 2–4, 1997 in Washington D.C., also brought national attention to the field of microenterprise. At the Summit, more than 2,000 people from over 100 nations gathered to launch a nine-year campaign to reach 100 million of the world's poorest families, with credit for self-employment and other financial services by the year 2000.[7]

In sum, efforts to support microbusinesses in the United States today attract support from a wide range of nonprofit organizations, community development corporations, community agencies, development banks and credit unions, the federal government, and the business and banking community.

B. The Importance of Microenterprise Development

The self-employment movement has a much greater impact than simply the number of microbusinesses created or assisted. Self-employment is an economic, human, family, and community development strategy that facilitates poverty reduction and encourages economic self-sufficiency, human dignity, and community empowerment. Neighborhood microbusinesses support individuals as well as families, and microentrepreneurs serve as community role models and create jobs.[8]

Poverty reduction is tied to American economic growth and competitiveness. It is not simply an economic issue; it is also a moral issue. Microenterprise development is an impressive intervention strategy that has the capacity to contribute much to poverty alleviation. Several re-

7. For more information contact RESULTS Education Fund (*see* Appendix) or visit the Microcredit Summit's Website at www.microcreditsummit.org.

8. *See* Lewis D. Solomon, *Microenterprise: Human Reconstruction in America's Inner Cities*, 15 Harv. J.L. & Pub. Pol'y 191, 191, 202 (1992).

cent studies illustrate this. For instance, an Aspen Institute study of 405 randomly selected microfinancing recipients revealed that:

- 83% are high school graduates;
- 78% are women;
- 62% are members of a minority group;
- 56% rely on microbusinesses as a primary source of income;
- 78% of their businesses survived for at least two years.[9]

Another study, conducted by the Self Employment Learning Project (SELP) of the Aspen Institute, showed 57% of microenterprises surviving after five years, with average revenues increasing 27% and profits doubling in that period. Furthermore, 72% of poor microenterpreneurs increased their household income over five years. And more than half—53%—of poor entrepreneurs moved over the poverty line.[10] A study of MED organizations found that five of seven microenterprise programs helped Aid to Families with Dependent Children (AFDC, now Temporary Assistance to Needy Families, TANF) recipients become self-sufficient. Of the entrepreneurs studied, 16% received AFDC and 48% received another public benefit such as food stamps, Supplemental Security Income (SSI), or general assistance (GA). Microenterprises allow low-wage families to have higher incomes than they would if members held only traditional wage employment.[11] Thus, self-employment is being used, in the aftermath of welfare reform, as a job creation strategy for welfare recipients and public housing tenants. In addition, self-employment can broaden options for persons with disabilities and the victims of domestic violence.[12]

Critics caution that microenterprise strategies will not cure poverty, nor will all entrepreneurs experience success.[13] In addition, critics point out that microenterprise programs, most of which operate as 501(c)(3)

---

9. *See* Mehta, *supra* note 6, at B2 (citing Self-Employment Learning Project, Aspen Institute, Microenterprise Assistance: What Are We Learning About Results (1995)).

10. AEO, Microenterprise Development in the U.S.—Economic Independence through Self Employment: Overview of a Successful Strategy, Microenterprise Fact Sheet, *available at* www.microenterpriseworks.org/about/factsheets/NewAEOMicroFactSheet2-Final10-03.pdf.

11. *See* Peggy Clark & Amy J. Kays, Aspen Institute, Enabling Entrepreneurship: Microenterprise Development in the United States 19, 21, 22, 24 (1995).

12. *See* Mehta, *supra* note 6 at B2.

13. Louise Howells, *The Dimensions of Microenterprise: A Critical Look at Microenterprise as a Tool to Alleviate Poverty*, 9 J. Affordable Hous. & Cmty. Dev. L. 2, 2000.

federally tax exempt organizations, are expensive to maintain and need donations to support operations, as do most other publically supported organizations. These skeptics also argue that it is difficult to grow a microbusiness into a stable small business, that microbusinesses do not create enough new jobs to revitalize poor communities, and that microbusinesses will collapse under the weight of formal legal regulations and tax compliance.[14] Although some of this may be true, microenterprise programs can make an extraordinary difference in the lives of some individuals. Microenterprise development programs may not achieve high success rates in every case, but industry studies show that they do work. The hard reality is that credit, the lifeblood of any economy, has largely dried up in America's inner cities.

C. Key Definitions[15]

Some of the terms used to refer to microenterprise programs can be confusing. The important terms are summarized below.[16]

- *Microenterprise or Microbusiness*: There is no standard definition of microenterprise; it is generally a very small business with few employees that usually does not have access to the commercial banking sector. A microenterprise usually needs a very small loan (between $500–$35,000) as start-up capital. AEO defines a microenterprise as a small business generally requiring $35,000 or less in start-up or expansion capital with five or fewer employees who are frequently related to each other. Many microenterprises—perhaps the majority—are businesses operated solely by the owner and his or her family, which has led to frequent use of the term self-employment (see below) in association with microenterprises. But microenterprises may also be established as corporations or

14. *See* Timothy M. Bates & Lisa Servon, *Why Loans Won't Work for the Poor,* INC., April 1, 1996, at 27, 27; *see also* First Lady Hillary Rodham Clinton, Remarks at the United Nations Fourth World Conference on Women (Sept. 6, 1995).

15. *See* Packet, *supra* note 3; *see also* Susan R. Jones, *Small Business and Community Economic Development; Transactional Lawyering for Social Change and Economic Justice,* 4 CLIN. L. REV. 195 (1997).

16. Contact the Association for Enterprise Opportunity (AEO) for a current glossary of Microenterprise Terms.

limited liability companies. The term microenterprise may also be used to refer to programs that help very small businesses.

- *Microenterprise Development (MED) Program*: A microenterprise development program, also called a microenterprise, microcredit or microloan program, is generally operated by a federally tax exempt nonprofit organization. The organization provides various services to microentrepreneurs in the form of credit, technical assistance, training, market access, economic literacy including asset development mechanisms such as individual development accounts (IDAs) and/or other business and personal assistance. Many domestic practitioners prefer the term microenterprise development because of its broader implications encompassing loans and education (and often a social service component). Many international models provide only loans without education and/or technical assistance (or they provide limited technical help); some of these models may be closer to a village-banking concept. The terminology used is often important to specific program models.
- *Microloan*: A microloan is a loan of $500 to $35,000 made to the very small businesses that are microenterprises. Maximum loan size varies across microenterprise programs, though the majority fall within the $15,000 to $25,000 range. Since they were established, the 198 lending programs profiled in the 2002 Microenterprise Directory have disbursed $213,879,591 in loans to microentrepreneurs.[17] The term "microloan program" is sometimes used to refer to a "microenterprise program." A microloan program usually provides straight loans sometimes without directly providing on-site education or technical assistance—although these components may be a prerequisite to obtaining a loan.
- *Microfinance, Microcredit and Microlending*: These terms are used interchangeably and refer to small loans. Microcredit is often used by international practitioners and is preferred by some over microfinance. Microfinance also refers to the broader array of financial services used by microenterprise programs, including assistance with credit repair, microloans, asset development activities such as IDAs (see below) or access to credit through credit unions or other community development financial institutions in the event the microenterprise program does not offer microloans in-house.

17. *See* 2002 Directory, *supra* note 5, at xviii.

- *Circle, Peer, or Group Lending*: These terms describe a lending method which involves forming groups who may guarantee each other's loans and help each other's businesses. The rationale is that peer pressure boosts repayment. Group members are expected to keep their loans current or members of the group will not be able to receive further loans.
- *Self-employment*: People who are self-employed work for 10 hours or more each week to earn a profit in a business they own. If this business is very small in terms of number of employees, sales, or assets, it is a microenterprise. The terms microenterprise and self-employment are used interchangeably, but they do not mean the same thing. Self-employment refers to the status of the business owner while microenterprise refers to a very small business itself.
- *Revolving Loan Funds (RLFs)*: An RLF is a pool of public and private funds that recycles money as the loans are repaid. They were first used for economic development purposes 20 years ago and are now well-established vehicles for ventures considered "risky" by conventional sources. Usually, RLFs are nonprofit organizations that lend to community-based projects, such as affordable housing developments and microenterprise programs.[18]
- *Individual Development Accounts (IDAs)*: IDAs are structured subsidized savings accounts for purposes such as education, home ownership, and microenterprise development. IDAs have been proposed as an antipoverty means to assist poor households in building assets through matching deposits. There is a three-prong strategy behind IDAs: (1) most people must save and invest if they are to leave poverty; (2) asset development and accumulation has a desirable impact on attitudes, behaviors, long-range planning, family stability, human capital, personal efficacy, community involvement, political participation, and social status; and (3) asset-holding has important intergenerational effects on the economic well-being and social behavior of children and other family members.[19]

---

18. *See* Steven D. Lyndenberg, *Alternative Loan Funds Support CED*, ECON. DEV. & L. CENTER REP., Sept./Oct. 1984, at 7; *see also Counting on Local Capital: A Research and Development Project for the Revolving Loan Fund (RLF) Industry*, AEO EXCHANGE, July 1997, at 4. The National Community Capital Association, listed in the Appendix, can also provide information on this subject.

19. *See* Will Marshall et al., Progressive Policy Institute Briefing, *Work First: A Proposal to Replace Welfare with an Employment System* (March 5, 1995), *available at* www.ppionline.org/ppi_ci.cfm?contentid=2089&knlgAreaID=114&subsecid=143 (last visited February 3, 2004).

D. Microenterprise Program Models

Microenterprise programs usually utilize different models, often referred to as "design elements" by microenterprise practitioners. These include entrepreneurial training and technical assistance, access to capital, access to new markets and asset development, and financial planning.

1. Entrepreneurial Training and Technical Support

Entrepreneurial training and support are traditional parts of enterprise development. Clients are provided with weeks or months of business training in areas such as management, marketing, accounting, bookkeeping, finance, legal issues, production, and sales. The business training usually includes one-on-one counseling and formal and informal training. Program success is measured by the number of enrollees completing the training, clients' mastery of business skills, and the number of participants who start small businesses. In some cases, loans may be available to program graduates.[20] Program success is measured in part by business formation and survival rates, but also by non-economic indicators such as participants' community involvement, attention to children's schooling, and acquisition of business or personal assets which are by-products of the training. Generally, all programs are urged to offer clients access to credit through innovative bank and other linkages if the program does not itself offer credit as a design component.

20. Some of these programs are Small Business Development Centers (SBDCs): The SBDC program of the Small Business Administration started in 1977 as a pilot program and was made permanent in 1980. This program provides counseling, training and specialized support assistance to the small business community . . . [and it] is implemented at the state and local level through 56 Small Business Development Centers and 1000 sub centers. The program's purpose is to provide technical assistance to improve the economic viability of small business in areas such as accounting, business planning, and related start-up or expansion matters. The objective of the SBDC program is to leverage funds with state, academic and private sector resources to strengthen the small business community, contribute to the economic growth of the communities served, create a broader based delivery system to the small business community, and make assistance available to more small businesses than is possible with present federal funds. Jones, *supra* note 14, at 23; Association of Small Business Development Centers, *at* www.asbdc-us.org (Last visited Jan. 9, 2004).

2. Access to Capital

Microenterprise development programs usually offer loan programs operated internally or accessed through a sister agency. Financial services have expanded to include asset development and financial planning.

3. Access to New Markets

This model may focus on a particular community or neighborhood and emphasizes improving the chances of introducing a business to the area and creating new markets beyond neighborhood borders. This feature of microenterprise development programs focuses on filling unmet consumer demands and minimizing displacement of existing business due to competition. Its success is measured by the number of new businesses. Examples of this may include franchise opportunities or the development of day care centers.

One aspect of creating access to new markets is cooperative or sectorial business development, a collective approach to enterprise development by selecting an industry or sector that has the potential to employ a large number of people (who are usually low-income) and forming a cooperatively owned enterprise in that industry (e.g., home health care or child care).[21] Another strategy is to network entrepreneurs who make similar products so that they might cooperatively seek new markets locally, regionally, nationally, and internationally. Cooperatives have a long history in the United States.[22] In the last decade, they have been used as a microenterprise model to create and preserve jobs, in-

21. *See* Peter Pitegoff, *Child Care Enterprise, Community Development and Work,* 81 GEO. L. J. 1897, 1897 (1993).

22. *See generally,* Scott L. Cummings, *Developing Cooperatives as a Job Creation Strategy for Low Income Workers,* 25 N.Y.U. REV. L. & SOC. CHANGE 181 (1999) (citing KIRK BAKER & ANTHONY NAKAZAWA, ORGANIZING FOR BUSINESS AS A COOPERATIVE (1995); ALASTAIR CAMPBELL, THE DEMOCRATIC CONTROL OF WORK (1969); CHRIS CORNFORTH ET AL., DEVELOPING SUCCESSFUL WORKER CO-OPERATIVES (1988); DAVID P. ELLERMAN, WHAT IS A WORKER COOPERATIVE? (1984); CHRISTOPHER GUNN, WORKERS' SELF-MANAGEMENT IN THE UNITED STATES (1984); GARY B. HANSEN, LESSONS FROM THE PAST: SELECTED READINGS ON THE SYSTEMATIC DEVELOPMENT OF WORKERS' COOPERATIVES TO GENERATE EMPLOYMENT AND INCOME (1993); GARY B. HANSEN & E. MOGENSEN, WORKING TOGETHER TO CREATE JOBS: A GUIDE TO WORKER-OWNED COOPERATIVE DEVELOPMENT (1994); PETER JAN HONIGSBERG ET AL., WE OWN IT (1991); LEN KRIMERMAN & FRANK LINDEFELD, WHEN WORKERS DECIDE: WORKPLACE DEMOCRACY TAKES ROOT IN NORTH

fluence industries to raise wages, and develop opportunities for business ownership by low-income people in their communities. Its success is measured by the number of jobs created, increased wage levels, increased number of employee-owned and employee-managed businesses, and their potential to influence specific industries.

4. Asset Development and Financial Planning

This feature focuses on the importance of using commercial checking and savings accounts to conduct financial transactions, the development of a credit history, savings clubs, IDA programs, and training on related topics such as civic responsibilities, tax responsibilities and voting.

These often integrated program design components converge and highlight several points. First, microenterprise is broader than offering microcredit. Lending is simply one strategy and a component of a larger, human development, and economic mission. Second, access to credit is important. If a microenterprise program does not offer credit in-house, it should have a relationship with a lender (e.g., revolving loan funds, banks, and credit unions); lending agencies can strengthen a program both substantively and by attracting clients. Third, in order to survive, microenterprise programs must consider assisting new clients to access new markets and create product innovations. Lastly, good legal counsel is indispensable to the development of the industry.

America (1992); Mary Meller et al., Worker Cooperatives in Theory and Practice (1988); Janet H. Saglio & J. Richard Hackman, The Design of Governance Systems for Small Worker Cooperatives (Industrial Cooperative Assoc. Working Paper, 1982); Worker Cooperatives in America (Robert Jackall & Henry M. Levin eds., 1984); Worker Ownership Development Foundation, Starting a Worker Co-operative: An Introduction (1985).

CHAPTER **2**

The Role of Lawyers in the Microenterprise Industry

A. Why Lawyers?

Microenterprise programs have successfully alleviated poverty for many low-income people, displaced workers, disabled people, Native Americans, and victims of domestic violence. Microenterprise practitioners indicate, however, that the rapid growth of the field may be outpacing the capacity to support it.[1] Microenterprise programs are complex and have sophisticated legal needs that can be met by business lawyers, banking specialists, and others in the legal community. For this reason, it is essential that attorneys volunteer to provide legal assistance to microenterprise programs and their clients.[2]

Business, legislative, banking, and other lawyers can play a critical role in supporting the microenterprise approach to economic development and poverty alleviation. Their skills can uniquely address the legal concerns of the programs that promote self-employment and the microentrepreneurs served by these programs. Microenterprise programs often require legal assistance with incorporating a nonprofit organization and obtaining federal and state tax exemption, expanding the work of an existing nonprofit group to include microenterprise

1. *See* Brad Caftel, *Helping Microenterprise Programs Succeed*, CED EXCHANGE, June 1993, at 1, 11.

2. *See* James L. Baillie, *Perspectives on Business Law: Fulfilling the Promise of Business Law Pro Bono* 28 WM. MITCHELL L. REV. 1543, 1547 (2002).

development, understanding lobbying restrictions, establishing sound loan documentation for microloans, debt collection, program financing, and fund raising. The microentrepreneurs often need assistance with choosing an appropriate legal entity, preparing contracts, securing business licenses or zoning permits, protecting inventions, and acquiring capital.

This book seeks to encourage and facilitate legal assistance to microenterprises. Specifically, it is designed to (1) provide legal guidance to attorneys who are not familiar with the microenterprise field and who want to represent microenterprises; (2) assist microenterprise practitioners with understanding the types of legal issues that may arise in their programs and the legal issues that microbusinesses may encounter; (3) provide legal guidance to attorneys who want to represent the small businesses assisted by microenterprise programs; and (4) identify legal resources that support microenterprise programs and microbusinesses.

There are many ways for lawyers to assist microenterprise programs and microbusinesses. But first, all lawyers should have a broad understanding of what they will encounter when dealing with microenterprise programs.

B. An Overview of Microenterprise Programs: Costs and Benefits[3]

It is important for lawyers who volunteer to work with microenterprise development programs and microbusinesses to have a broad understanding of their purposes and activities. One important element of microenterprise development programs is to provide credit in the form of microloans, or to provide access to credit by identifying ways to obtain loans, such as through a bank that works with the microenterprise program. There are programs that provide credit and an in-depth business education. Others, however, offer borrowers only limited technical assistance and training. These latter programs often have relationships with banks, credit unions, and other lenders.

3. Peter Manzo drafted portions of this section.

1. Costs

One of the first issues lawyers, bankers, and others encounter is that microenterprise programs are fairly expensive and require a range of resources to operate soundly. This is true of most other community economic development programs with a service mission. When viewed simply in terms of the number and dollar amount of loans made in a given year and compared to the operating costs of the program to support those loans, microenterprise programs may even appear wasteful. It is not uncommon for microenterprise programs to make an average of one-to-two loans per month, or fewer, at an average cost of two dollars in operating costs for every dollar loaned. Indeed, many microenterprise practitioners would be quite pleased with a dollar-for-dollar cost of making microloans and a volume of one-to-two loans per month.

Faced with these facts alone, a board member of a Los Angeles based microenterprise program asked: "Instead of investing so much effort and time into microenterprise programs, why don't we just hire a helicopter, fly over the target neighborhoods, and throw the money out of the window?" As a retired accountant with extensive experience in helping businesses of all sizes, this observer initially questioned the value of such programs. But, after seeing firsthand the broad range of impact that the microenterprise program had on individuals, especially in developing "human capital" (including self-esteem, confidence, and the drive to obtain financial self-sufficiency[4]), this same board member became an enthusiastic convert and advocate for the mission of the program. Ultimately, he became the chairperson of the microenterprise board.

Thus, the numbers do not tell the whole story. The success of microenterprise programs cannot be assessed solely by the number or the amount of the loans and the cost of making these loans. Microenterprise programs pursue several ends including poverty alleviation, business and economic development, job creation, and human development.[5]

4. Human capital refers to the education, skill level, and problem solving abilities that will enable an individual to be a productive worker in the global economy of the 21st century. *See* Theodore Hershberg, *Human Capital Development: America's Greatest Challenge*, 544 Annals Am. Acad. Pol. & Soc. Sci. 43, 44 (1996).

5. *See* Caftel, *supra* note 22, at 2.

2. Benefits of Microenterprise Programs: Evaluating Program Success

Microenterprise clients benefit from the many successful outcomes that microenterprise development programs inspire. Some may learn skills such as planning, cash flow management, employee hiring and personnel issues, and communication skills that will make their business venture stronger, make them more employable by others, or simply provide a sounder footing for households. Other clients may receive a microloan and start a successful new business or expand an existing one. In some instances, comprehensive business planning, counseling, and financial advice may enable some clients to get a loan from a commercial bank. Some individuals may decide not to start their own businesses, but if the client makes an informed decision about the risks involved and avoids a possible business failure, this, too, is a success—especially when that individual has acquired business training and goes on to make a better employment choice. And on the flip side, when an individual gains the knowledge and confidence to realize that starting a business will not work, this realization is also an important victory for the individual.

3. Adding Up Costs and Benefits: Characteristics of Successful Microenterprise Programs[6]

Loan loss rates must not be the only measure of success for microenterprise programs. Successful microenterprise programs must be accessible to the populations they serve. For instance, they might conduct training and outreach in community settings ideally accessible by public transportation. Successful programs should also be affordable, but not free—it is important to the concept of microenterprise development that it not be viewed as charity. Targeting diverse communities, programs should generally seek and accept clients from low-income to moderate-income, including dislocated workers, disabled persons, minorities, women, and others. In addition, they should engage clients in

6. This section is based on Peter Manzo's interview with Mari Riddle, former Executive Director of the Center for Women's Economic Development.

a constant self-assessment of their skills, including their ability to run the microbusiness, understanding the market or customer base, and the financial viability of the business. Some programs geared toward low-income people also ensure that training materials are written simply so that they are understandable to those who lack formal education or are learning the English language and/or American business customs. Programs targeting immigrants and refugees should ensure that their materials are translated into the appropriate language.

Armed with this overview of the fundamental nature of microenterprise development programs, lawyers can then begin to provide them with practical help.

C. Getting Started: How Lawyers Can Get Involved in Microenterprise Programs and Microbusinesses[7]

Lawyers should first consult the most recent Directory of U.S. Microenterprise Programs or contact AEO for an up to date listing of programs in their community.[8] In addition, community outreach activities are an excellent way to identify microenterprise clients and for lawyers to become involved in transactional work for microentrepreneurs. Lawyers should develop relationships with microenterprise practitioners; however, they should avoid relying on microenterprise program staff to refer their clients for legal assistance because non-lawyer staff members may not always recognize legal issues. Moreover, borrowers often are hesitant to mention potential legal problems to program staff from whom they have received or expect to receive a loan. Microentrepreneurs themselves, of course, may also overlook important legal concerns. It is essential, then, for attorneys seeking to help microbusinesses to try to reach microbusiness program clients directly, perhaps through educational seminars and legal clinic hours at microenterprise program offices. Bar associations, public interest groups, legal services organizations, law school legal clinics, and pro bono programs can organize and

7. Andrea Ball and Peter Manzo drafted portions of this section.
8. *See* 2002 Directory, *supra* note 5, passim.

host workshops and place individual attorneys who are interested in doing pro bono work with microentrepreneurs and microenterprise programs.

Lawyers can also give talks and conduct seminars about elementary business considerations, answer basic questions, and help microentrepreneurs who have specific questions. The greatest demand among microenterprise borrowers is for essential information such as what a lawyer can do for them and whether they can negotiate fees. Borrowers also need help reviewing leases and contracts.

Finally, lawyers must understand the legal, statutory, and regulatory authority for microloans and technical assistance funds such as the Community Development Block Grant Program (CBDG), which now recognizes microentrepreneurs as an appropriate beneficiary class to which CDBG funds can be provided.

25 Things Lawyers Can Do for Microenterprise Programs

1. Serve on the Board of Directors or on the Advisory Board for the purpose of assisting programs in standards aspects of the business operation
2. Serve as general counsel
3. Educate the banks and other financial institutions who are their clients about microenterprise development
4. Share this book with a friend or colleague
5. Make socially conscious investments that support microenterprise development
6. Advocate to ensure that microenterprise development is part of their state's welfare plans and job creation strategy
7. Teach microenterprise technical assistance classes on choice of legal entity, licensing, bonding, insurance, contracts, etc.
8. Determine if a microenterprise statewide network exists in their state
9. Write articles on legal issues of importance to microenterprise programs and microentrepreneurs
10. Provide legal assistance to new microenterprise organizations in acquiring federal, state, and local tax exemption and in drafting the organization's nonprofit articles of incorporation and bylaws
11. Counsel programs whose nonprofit status could be jeopardized by work that may be legally classified as for-profit business such as operating a manufacturing concern or a retail business

12. Explore the possibilities of establishing holding companies and other non-501(c)(3) organizations
13. Establish sound documentation of loan agreements, promissory notes, peer group responsibilities, and other issues of concern to lenders
14. Assist in financing the microenterprise activities through grants and program-related investments and loan guarantees through local banks
15. Advise programs in the collection process including enforcement of promissory notes and cases in small-claims court
16. Serve on loan review committees that help advise program staff on making sound lending decisions
17. Advise programs on board member liability, responsibilities of directors, staff, loan committees, and liability to outside volunteers and contractors and assist in the preparation of comprehensive employee and volunteer policy and procedure manuals
18. Prepare or review supplier contracts and other agreements
19. Perform legal "check-ups" of microenterprise programs by reviewing operational matters such as record keeping and reporting for tax and employment law purposes
20. Provide personal legal assistance that is unrelated to the microentrepreneur's business but which may threaten it, such as landlord-tenant, credit and consumer issues
21. Help microenterprise programs understand the application of state regulations and laws affecting MED and the application of federal bankruptcy laws
22. Assist microenterprise programs in interpreting lending laws and other federal statutes such as The Truth in Lending Act and The Equal Opportunity Credit Act
23. Represent self-employment associations (or groups of borrowers)
24. Legal Services and other lawyers familiar with Temporary Assistance to Needy Families (TANF) can assist TANF recipients and the MED programs that aid them[9]
25. Consult with microenterprise programs considering merger or dissolution

---

9. *See generally* www.clasp.org (last visited Feb. 8, 2004). The Center for Law and Social Policy (CLASP), a national non-profit organization founded in 1968, conducts research, policy analysis, technical assistance, and advocacy on issues related to economic security for low-income families with children. In addition, CLASP is a leader in the national effort to establish equal justice for all.

D. Lawyers Assisting Microenterprise Programs and Their Clients: Examples from the Field

As mentioned above, lawyers can assist microenterprise programs and their clients in a variety of ways. Legal assistance to microenterprise programs has included:

- Developing loan agreements and security documents for borrowers to use;
- Advising a large and successful microenterprise program on dissolution;
- Advising and assisting with collection procedures—an unfortunate but necessary component of program survival and stability;
- Advising programs on board member liability, responsibilities of directors, staff, loan committees, and liability to outside volunteers;
- Assistance with restructuring and merging microenterprise programs.

Some particular examples from around the nation are discussed below.

1. The East Coast

In Boston and New York, lawyers conducted workshops on representing inner city entrepreneurs and microbusinesses.[10]

A New York law firm, assigned to work with a microenterprise development organization through New York Lawyers for the Public Interest, helped microentrepreneurs by conducting workshops on topics ranging from legal compliance to loan applications.

In Washington, D.C., lawyers prepared corporate documents for a women-owned construction contracting business, wrote contracts for

10. Goodwin Procter in Boston conducted Open for Business: Workshop on Representing Inner City Entrepreneurs on February 12, 2004 (materials on file with the author). Paul Weiss held a workshop, Representing Microbusinesses (materials on file with the author).

party decorators and wedding planners, and taught microenterprise program training classes on insurance and bonding as well as the process for obtaining business licenses and permits.

2. The West Coast

In California, a lawyer advised a service company on converting the status of its workers from independent contractors to employees.

In Los Angeles an attorney helped a woman who made earthquake survival kits for children to negotiate a contract with a salesperson to market and distribute her kits.[11]

Lawyers have also been instrumental in restructuring a partnership to operate a hair salon in Oakland, California; assisting a tenant association in forming a joint venture for a prominent Los Angeles nonprofit organization to develop a resident-owned construction company; and providing a nonprofit organization with assistance regarding the equity investment of a new small business that offered job training and employment opportunities for residents of South Los Angeles.

3. The Midwest and Mountain States

The Women's Self-Employment Project (WSEP) in Chicago has partnered with the Community Economic Development Law Project (CEDL). WSEP refers clients to the CEDL, and the CEDL conducts workshops on the legal aspects of starting a microbusiness.

In coordination with the Colorado State Microenterprise Association, the Colorado Lawyers Committee conducts quarterly "Business Law Workshops" to help build the capacity of microentrepreneurs and to address related legal issues.[12]

A lawyer in Missouri assisted the Microenterprise Development Program International Institute of St. Louis by developing a checklist of

11. Andrea Ball and Pete Manzo provided this example.

12. Email from Melissa Scudo, Executive Director, Colorado Alliance for Microenterprise Initiative (CAMI) and director of the State Microenterprise Association in Colorado (July 15, 2003) (on file with the author).

questions to ask a landlord and a lease rider to protect the business if the leased premises did not pass a safety inspection.[13] The lawyer also represented a microentrepreneur in a legal action to recover a commercial lease deposit and first month's rent when the building failed to pass a safety inspection.

4. *Nationwide*

Other efforts have occurred nationally, such as with the establishment of Microenterprise Legal Clinics in cities such as San Francisco, Chicago, Boston and Washington, D.C.

Also, law school legal clinics focused on small business and community economic development have also provided legal help to new microenterprise programs, job training and apprenticeship programs, and a wide range of individual microentrepreneurs.[14]

E. Lawyers Can Help Microbusinesses, the Clients of Microenterprise Development Programs

In addition to helping the nonprofit entities that provide technical assistance to microbusinesses, lawyers can help individual microentrepreneurs. As demonstrated below, lawyers are uniquely qualified to provide

13. Email from Mary Fischer-Gobble, Senior Business Development Specialist, Microenterprise Development Program International Institute of St. Louis (July 15, 2003) (on file with the author).

14. *See* A BUSINESS COMMITMENT *available at* www.abanet.org/buslaw/probono/abc/abc.pdf; Nora R. Kelly, *Small Step-Up: Microloans*, GEO. WASH. U. MAG., June 1994, at 21; *see also* Leslie Newman, *Law Schools Building a Corps of Lawyers Skilled in CED, in* NATIONAL ECONOMIC DEVELOPMENT & LAW CENTER, COUNSELING ORGANIZATIONS IN COMMUNITY ECONOMIC DEVELOPMENT 1-20c, 1-20c (1994); Jeffrey S. Lehman & Rochelle E. Lento, *Law School Support for Community-Based Economic Development in Low Income Urban Neighborhoods*, 42 J. URB. & CONTEMP. L. 65, 66 (1992); Peter Pitegoff, *Law School Initiatives in Housing and Community Development*, 4 B.U. PUB. INT. L.J. 275, 276 (1995); Susan R. Jones, *Small Business and Community Economic Development: Transactional Lawyering for Social Change and Economic Justice*, 4 Clm. Rev. 195 (1997).

microenterprise programs and their clients with valuable problem-solving information.

Lawyers can:

- Assist the microentrepreneur in determining the best form for doing business, structuring the relationship and creating the entity, e.g., partnership, corporation, limited liability company, sole proprietorship;
- Name a business or product including obtaining a federal trademark, or service mark, or obtaining a federal or state trademark;
- Determine whether the business must obtain a license or permit and help the business to secure the appropriate one;
- Address zoning issues for home-based businesses and other types of enterprises;
- Assist with legal tax matters such as obtaining an employer identification number, becoming an S corporation, understanding basic business taxes and deductions, and the differences between classifying workers as independent contractors or employees;
- Help determine ways to raise capital or assist microentrepreneurs with buying or selling a business, due diligence, valuing the business, drafting the letter of intent to purchase and conducting the closing;
- Interpret franchise agreements;
- Negotiate favorable leases and provide counsel on various types of insurance;
- Draft and interpret contracts;
- Review and interpret loan documents.

F. Legal and Business Checklist for Lawyers Working with Microentrepreneurs and Microbusinesses

The lists below provide a basic checklist of legal and business issues and sample interview questions to help facilitate attorney involvement with microenterprise programs and their clients. Lawyers contemplating work in this area should find both lists helpful.

Preliminary Interview Questions

Does the client have a written business plan?	yes	no
If so, have you read it?	yes	no
Does the client have a resume?	yes	no
If so, have you read it?	yes	no

Can you identify legal issues after reviewing the business plan or talking with the client? If so, list them:

Where will the business be located? (fill in city, county and state).

Will the business operate in more than one city, county or state? If so, you may need to perform additional legal work such as qualifying a domestic corporation to operate as a foreign corporation or obtain licenses and permits for all jurisdictions in which the business will operate.

Areas of the Client's Legal Need or Assistance to Be Checked

General:

Legal consultation to determine needs. In addition to obtaining relevant facts, remember that all good legal consultations also serve the purpose of building rapport with the client.

Choice of Entity:

Sole Proprietorship
General Partnership
Limited Partnership
Limited Liability Limited Partnership
Corporation—C Corporation
S Corporation
Professional Corporation
Limited Liability Company
Professional Limited Liability Company
Nonprofit Corporation
Federal Tax Exemption for Nonprofit Corporation

Contracts:

Commercial Lease Agreement
Employment Contract
Service Contract

Franchise or License Agreement
Other type of contract: specify (examples include independent contractor agreement, sales contract, consulting agreement)

Licenses or Permits:

License: type (if known)
Permit: type (if known)

NOTE: Call the local business regulation department and visit the website to determine whether the client needs a license or permit for businesses such as home improvement, day care, beauty and barbershops, etc. It is very important to verify whether a license is needed. This information changes periodically and business activities not previously regulated may become regulated industries.

Intellectual Property:

Copyright
Trademark
Patent
Other issues:
Royalty
Licenses

Taxes:

Employer Identification Number
Quarterly tax payments
Other: specify

Insurance:

General Liability
Home Office Rider to Homeowner's Insurance
Malpractice

Bonds:

Fidelity Bonds

Other Legal Issues to Be Researched:

Specify

Sample Interview Questions to Ask Microbusiness Clients

1. What kind of business are you going into?
2. Have you obtained a license or permit to operate it?
3. Are you already in business?
4. Have you been employed in a business that is the same or similar to the one you are in?
5. How long have you been in business?
6. How many people (workers) are involved in your business?
7. Where will the business be primarily located (city, county, state)?
8. Do you plan to operate the business out of your home?[15]
9. If you plan to operate the business out of your home, do you have a license or permit to do this?
10. Are there any restrictions on operating a home business in your lease agreement?
11. Have you established a legal entity for your business such as a partnership, limited liability company, corporation or sole proprietorship?
12. Do you have an Employer Identification Number (EIN)?
13. Do you have insurance? If so, what type(s)?
14. Do you have workers compensation insurance?
15. Do you have particular legal questions or concerns about running your small business? If so, what are they?

The issues and questions in the above lists are the kind that lawyers need to be concerned with when they are helping microenterprise programs and their clients. The following sections of this book outline more specific issues and concerns that lawyers must confront in dealing with microenterprise development programs.

15. *See* Margaret Beebe Held, *Developing Microbusinesses in Public Housing: Notes From the Field,* 31 Harv. C.R.-C.L. L. Rev. 473 (1996).

CHAPTER **3**

Legal Formation Issues for Microenterprise Programs

There are exacting and complex issues for lawyers to consider in forming or dealing with microenterprise programs. The following sections provide an overview of specific issues and how lawyers can get started in addressing them.

A. Establishing a Microenterprise Development Program: Legal Organization

A group that is interested in starting a microenterprise program must first determine how it will be legally organized. Will the entity be a for-profit or nonprofit enterprise? Will it be a corporation or some other legal entity? Because the goals of microenterprise programs are to foster economic development and alleviate poverty, the nonprofit form is probably most appropriate. In fact, most microenterprise development programs are organized as tax-exempt organizations under section 501(c)(3) of the Internal Revenue Code (IRC), as charitable or educational organizations.[1] In addition, microenterprise programs are usually

1. A few may be organized under I.R.C. § 501(c)(4) as tax-exempt social welfare organizations. As its name implies, it must engage in social welfare activities which will benefit a community rather than a select group of individuals. Although 501(c)(4) social welfare organizations and 501(c)(3) charitable organizations are similar in many respects, there are notable differences. For example, a social welfare organization cannot attract charitable contributions that are deductible for income, gift, and estate tax purposes and can engage in substantial lobbying. *See* Bruce R.

nonprofit corporations chartered under the laws of the state in which the program operates and are thus exempt from state tax.

More than 750 nonprofit microenterprise programs (including MED support organizations) exist around the country and their organizing documents should serve as a guide for new organizations.[2] In working with a new microenterprise program, a lawyer should first examine the state nonprofit corporation law and prepare and file articles of incorporation with the state. The articles of incorporation should set out corporate purposes that are consistent with the state and federal tax status that the organization is seeking. Other organizing documents, such as by-laws and organizational minutes,[3] will also be needed.

Many new microenterprise programs will choose to become a nonprofit corporation and obtain federal tax exemption. An existing organization has two options: (1) incorporate as a separate nonprofit corporation and obtain federal and local tax exemption or (2) become part of an existing 501(c)(3) organization, making sure that its activities are educational and/or charitable, and advising the IRS of the expanded purposes of the existing 501(c)(3) organization.[4]

A new microenterprise program might want to consider incubating within an existing organization. It could then eventually spin off on its own or remain a division of the existing organization, depending on which choice offers more advantages. For example, Jubilee Jobs (JJ) is a non-profit employment service in Washington, D.C., that locates entry level jobs for the inner-city poor, the homeless, recovering substance abusers, ex-offenders, and recent immigrants.[5] Since 1981, JJ has placed over 13,000 persons in permanent employment. Nevertheless, most of these jobs pay only minimum wage and individuals and families are still struggling to survive. In 1994, hoping to facilitate economic self-sufficiency, JJ created The Barnabas Self-Employment Project. The first D.C. microenterprise program, Barnabas was a pilot project designed to help inner-city residents supplement their family income by providing limited credit, business training and moral col-

---

Hopkins, The Law of Tax Exempt Organizations 551-52 (1996); Bruce R. Hopkins, Nonprofit Law Dictionary 300 (1994).

2. *See* Friedman & Sahay, *supra* note 5.

3. *See* Barbara Kirschten, Nonprofit Corporation Forms Handbook (2003).

4. The group may decide to become an unincorporated association and seek federal tax exemption, but the unincorporated association will not have the limited liability that the corporate form affords.

5. *See* www.jubileejobs.org/index.htm (last visited Feb. 13, 2004).

lateral. After careful legal analysis, the Barnabas organizers decided that it was better for Barnabas to remain a division of JJ instead of spinning off on its own.

Legal counsel is very important when deciding whether to form a new entity or operate as part of an existing entity. Consideration of the following questions may assist in making the determination:

- Is the microenterprise effort a pilot program (temporary or experimental)?
- How will it be funded?
- Will the microenterprise program be an integral part of the work of the organization?
- What model(s) or design components of microlending will the group use?
- Is it possible that the liabilities from one part of the organization's work could flow through to the work of the microenterprise development program or vice versa?
- Has the existing organization encountered legal problems in the past which would influence this decision?
- Has someone ever sued the existing organization?
- How much risk is associated with adding the microenterprise program?
- Does the organization have general liability insurance?

Taking these issues into account, as well as any others that arise, will help determine what legal status is best for an entity.

B. Federal Tax Exemption Overview

In order to obtain federal tax exemption as a 501(c)(3) entity, the entity must be "organized and operated exclusively for . . . charitable . . . or educational purposes."[6] The term "charitable" as used in the Internal Revenue Code includes relief of the poor and distressed or of the underprivileged, advancement of education, and promotion of social welfare through organizations formed to lessen neighborhood tensions,

6. I.R.C. § 501(c)(3) (1986).

eliminate prejudice and discrimination, or combat community deterioration or juvenile delinquency.[7] Donors can deduct contributions made to a 501(c)(3) charitable organization. Funding sources will often only give money to organizations that have received 501(c)(3) federal tax exemption from the Internal Revenue Service (IRS).

The request for federal tax exemption under section 501(c)(3) is made on IRS Form 1023, Application for Recognition of Exemption. IRS Publication No. 557, *Tax-Exempt Status for Your Organization*, is a helpful guide.[8] The Appendix of this book also contains a bibliography of resources on nonprofit legal and management issues. Several of the publications in that section contain sample tax exemption applications and other important information about the application process.

Lawyers working with microenterprise programs should also review the relevant IRS Rulings.[9] A microenterprise program may operate as a tax-exempt organization if the objective of the program is the promotion of social welfare, the loan recipients are unable to obtain loans from commercial sources, the loans are made solely to members of minority or disadvantaged groups, and the individuals reside in economically depressed areas and operate their businesses in such areas.[10]

Some of the permissible purposes of a microenterprise program are to:

- Operate a microenterprise program designed to stimulate economic development in urban areas inhabited by low-income minorities or other disadvantaged groups;
- Decrease social unrest and instability of the serviced area;
- Elevate the depressed economic market of the serviced community;
- Provide entrepreneurial training and employment opportunities to unemployed and under-employed residents;

---

7. *See* Treas. Reg. § 1.501(c)(3)-1(d)(2) (1997).

8. *See* Internal Revenue Service, U.S. Dep't of the Treasury, Publication No. 557, Tax-Exempt Status for Your Organization (Rev'd 2003), available at www.irs.gov/pub/irs-pdf/p557.pdf (last visited Apr. 19, 2004).

9. *See* Rev. Rul. 74-587, 1974-2 C.B. 162; *see also* Gen. Couns. Mem. 38,826 (March 10, 1982). In addition, the author has found the following sources especially helpful: Jody Blazek, Tax Planning and Compliance for Tax Exempt Organizations: Forms, Checklists, Procedures (4th ed. 2004); Brad Caftel et al., National Economic Development and Law Center, Counseling Organizations in Community Economic Development (1994); Bruce R. Hopkins, The Law of Tax-Exempt Organizations, 8th ed. (2003).

10. *See* A. Jan Behrsin, What is the IRS' Position on Exemptions for Business Development Organizations?, Nat'l Econ. Dev. L. Project Rep., Mar./Apr. 1978, at 3–25; see generally Michael I. Sanders Hot Issues Affecting Partnerships and Joint Ventures Involving Non-Profits, 20 Exempt Org. Tax Rev. 93 (1998).

- Assist in the creation of small businesses using unskilled or inexperienced local workers;
- Use local suppliers in microenterprises who will become directly involved in community affairs;
- Encourage residents and young people to search for legal means to earn a living and to improve themselves;
- Serve as a role model of self-sufficiency to other community residents and young people;
- Provide positive role models for community entrepreneurship;
- Aid minority-owned businesses by promoting the social welfare of the community and by helping to lessen prejudice and discrimination against minority groups by teaching self-employment concepts and creating self-help opportunities;
- Relieve poverty while at the same time lessening neighborhood tensions and dissatisfaction arising from the lack of employment opportunities by facilitating the rejuvenation of businesses that will provide a means of livelihood and expanded job opportunities for unemployed and underemployed people in the community;
- Combat community deterioration by helping to establish viable enterprises in the area.[11]

C. State or Local Tax Exemption

A nonprofit organization probably may need to obtain a state tax exemption. This may mean giving the state a copy of the federal tax exemption approval or it may mean filing a separate application. Reviewing the state regulations will clarify what to do in each case.

D. Licenses and Permits Needed by Microenterprise Programs

The next consideration is whether the organization will need a state or county license or permit to operate in the jurisdiction. Examples of the

11. *See id.*

types of license that may be needed are a Money Lender's License[12] (for businesses loaning over a specified amount of money) or a Charitable Solicitation License[13] (for fund raising). Call the business regulations authority to determine whether the organizations will need a license of some kind. General information about business regulation may be obtained from any local Chamber of Commerce.[14]

E. Insurance for Microenterprise Programs

A nonprofit microenterprise program should have various types of insurance to protect it. The most important types of insurance are (1) Officers' and Directors' Insurance; (2) Workers' Compensation Insurance; and (3) General Liability Insurance.

1. Officers' and Directors' Insurance

People who volunteer to serve on nonprofit boards have fiduciary responsibilities, including the duty of special trust (to act honestly and fairly); duty of care (attending meetings, exercising independent business judgment in the best interests of the organization); and duty of loyalty (understanding the mission and function of the nonprofit organization and avoiding conflicts of interests).[15] Moreover, board members have important responsibilities for setting policy and overseeing the organization. While performing these volunteer activities, the board is also exposed to risks associated with operating a nonprofit "business" such as employment laws and regulations. Each board member can be held personally liable for the wrongful acts of the association.[16] For this

12. *See, e.g.*, D.C. Code Ann. § 29-901 (2001), which requires a money lender's license for any business loaning money upon which a rate of interest greater than 6% per annum is charged on any security of any kind; microlending activity is not exempt.

13. D.C. Code §§ 44-1701 to 44-1714 (2001). The law requires a license for charitable solicitations which include direct or indirect requests for contributions, oral and written.

14. See www.Chamber-of-Commerce.com or the Small Business Administration (see Appendix).

15. *See* Brad J. Caftel, *The Responsibilities of Nonprofit Board Members*, ECON. DEV. & L. CENTER REP., March/April 1984, at 20, 22.

16. *See* Donald G. Kempf, Jr., "*Can They Really Take My House?*" *Defending Directors and Officers*, 81 ILL. B.J. 244, 244 (1993).

reason, Directors' and Officers' (D & O) insurance should be obtained to protect against financial and management malpractice. For new organizations, the cost of this insurance can be as low as $800 a year.[17]

2. Workers' Compensation and Unemployment Insurance

Workers' compensation insurance, which covers the employer's liability for injuries received by employees on the job, is important for microenterprise programs and for microenterprise businesses and may be required by state law. Workers' compensation insurance covers an employee regardless of whether the employer was negligent and most states allow for workers' compensation so long as the injury occurred in the course of employment. The amount of money that an employee can collect is usually limited to medical treatment, lost wages, and impaired future earnings. State law governs workers' compensation, and insurance is issued by a state fund or private insurance agents. In some areas, the state funds workers' compensation insurance. Sometimes larger employers will self-insure. Industry, occupation, or the size of the payroll determines rates for workers' compensation.

State laws generally require employers to pay unemployment insurance. The purpose of this insurance is to compensate workers who lose their jobs because of cutbacks or other involuntary reasons. The rate for this insurance is based on a number of factors including the size of the payroll.[18]

3. General Liability and Other Insurance

A general liability policy is designed to protect microenterprise programs against a host of common perils. For instance, a guest may slip

---

17. *See* Committee on Nonprofit Corporations, AMERICAN BAR ASSOCIATION SECTION OF BUSINESS LAW, GUIDEBOOK FOR DIRECTORS OF NONPROFIT CORPORATIONS, 2D ED. (2002). Contact a local insurance broker or Nonprofit Mutual Risk Retention Group, Inc. 125 Airport Road, Concord, NH 03301.

18. *See* FRED S. STEINGOLD, THE LEGAL GUIDE FOR STARTING AND RUNNING A SMALL BUSINESS 13/22 (1995).

and fall. This type of insurance policy protects the business against lawsuits, money judgments, and other damages up to the amount of the policy limit and the costs of legal defense.

Microenterprise programs should identify a knowledgeable insurance agent who will take the time to analyze the program's needs and possible liabilities. Other insurance priorities may include property, fire and hazard, real estate, vehicles, and employee bonds. Legal counsel can play a critical role in reviewing and interpreting insurance policies.[19]

F. Lender Liability

The greatest exposure lenders face from borrowers is a claim (raised either in defense to collection or foreclosure actions by the lender, or at the borrower's initiative) that the lender's actions caused the borrower's business to falter and default on the loan, through the lender's involvement in the borrower's business decisions, such as approving or disapproving expenditures by the borrower, perhaps even suggesting or requiring changes in management personnel and the like. As a practical matter, this risk is virtually unavoidable for microenterprise assistance programs that provide a substantial amount of technical assistance both prior to and during the term of a loan.[20]

Although microenterprise assistance programs risk being sued by individual microentrepreneurs, these instances are rare because lender liability lawsuits are rare. The most likely kinds of lawsuits involve claims of discrimination in lending, common tort negligence, breach of contract, and interference with business relations. However, other suits can occur. In one instance, a microenterprise program asked legal counsel to investigate its liability in the event one member of a borrowing group took physical action against another member who had defaulted. Absent additional facts, it appeared that the microenterprise program did not face legal liability for a criminal and/or civil assault and battery by one microenterprise participant against another.

Other institutions that lend money, such as credit unions, banks, and groups that provide hands-on technical assistance and training to

19. *See id.* at 22/1.

20. *See, e.g.*, Jay Finegan, "Banker's Suits," Inc., Nov. 1989, available at www.inc.com/magazine/19891101/5875.html (last visited Apr. 19, 2004).

microbusinesses also face risk of being sued. In all instances, the best way to protect against these types of claims may be to obtain insurance.

G. Credit Reports and Credit Practices

Microenterprise programs must understand consumer laws relevant to credit reports and credit practices. Enforced by the Federal Trade Commission, these laws are designed to protect consumers. They are generally very complex and require businesses that offer credit, including microloans, to state such details as the applicable interest charges. These details must be worded in a particular manner and typed in a way that is clear and conspicuous.

The statutes of primary concern to microenterprise programs are:[21]

- The Truth in Lending Act, which contains information about computing the annual percentage rate and the way documents describe the lending rate;[22]
- The Equal Credit Opportunity Act, which was enacted to ensure that women have equal access to credit regardless of their marital status;[23]
- The Fair Credit Billing Act, which describes how to deal with complaints about bills sent by businesses to customers;[24]
- The Fair Debt Collection Practices Act, which describes appropriate and inappropriate procedures when attempting to collect unpaid debts from consumers;[25]
- The Fair Credit Reporting Act which gives consumers the right to see their credit file and correct inaccurate information which may affect their ability to obtain credit;[26] and
- State usury laws.

The U.S. Federal Trade Commission (FTC) has useful information on these topics and will also provide copies of the laws upon request.[27]

21. Some of these, however, may not apply to loans for business purposes.
22. 15 U.S.C. §§ 1601–1667f as amended (2000).
23. 15 U.S.C. §§ 1691–1691f as amended (2000).
24. 15 U.S.C. §§ 1666–1666j.
25. 15 U.S.C. §§ 1692–1692o as amended (2000).
26. 15 U.S.C. §§ 1681–1681u as amended (2000).
27. Write the Federal Trade Commission at FTC, Public Reference Branch, 6th and Pennsylvania, NW, Room 130, Washington, D.C. 20580 or call (202) 326-2222.

Also, microenterprise practitioners have reported that a good starting place for understanding credit reports and credit practices is Highlights of the Fair Credit Reporting Act for Credit Granters and Consumers, Credit Bureaus and the Fair Credit Reporting Act.[28]

H. Loan Agreements, Promissory Notes, Contracts and Collateral[29]

A loan agreement and promissory note should evidence the loan to a microenterprise participant. These are contracts between the borrower and the lender. Some microenterprise programs require collateral in order for the microbusiness to receive the loan. Collateral is property, such as a house or business inventory, to secure the loan. Because many microbusinesses do not have these types of assets, some programs permit participants to use non-traditional collateral such as jewelry or bicycles. Alternatively, group lending provides "moral collateral."

Lawyers who draft loan applications and agreements for microenterprise programs should consider the following matters.

- *The Loan Application*: The loan application should request all material information that will be required of the borrower prior to the loan disbursement, including the borrower's name, permanent address, sources of income, asset and debt information, credit history, and the proposed use of the loan proceeds. The information provided in the loan application must be sufficient to allow the lender to assess whether the borrower can expect sufficient business profit to repay interest and principal within a timely period. The loan agreement should also include language requiring the borrower to represent and warrant that the information contained in the loan application is true and accurate as of the date of the loan agreement and that any change in the information will be reported.

---

28. The Associated Credit Bureaus, Inc., 1090 Vermont Avenue, N.W., Suite 200, Washington, D.C. 20005-4905 (www.acb-credit.com) publishes both of these pamphlets. For more information, visit the Federal Trade Commission's Bureau of Consumer Protection Website at www.ftc.gov/bcp.html.

29. David Dedyo drafted the section regarding loan agreements.

- *Lender of Last Resort*: Microenterprise lenders are frequently lenders of last resort for low-income borrowers who usually do not qualify for conventional loans. To ensure that the microenterprise is, in fact, creditworthy, a program may wish to require that a borrower has undertaken and exhausted other efforts to obtain bank or other conventional financing before disbursing a loan. For instance, they could require the loan applicant to list on the loan application form all other sources from which they have sought financing for their proposed projects, in what dollar amounts, and whether the financing was approved or denied. Some programs provide credit rehabilitation services.
- *The Loan Agreement*: The specific terms of each microenterprise loan will vary on a case-by-case basis. In general, a microenterprise lender should establish maximum loan amounts and maturity limits. Making a succession of small loans available to a borrower as each previous loan is successfully repaid can accommodate demand for loans that exceed the maximum amounts established by a microenterprise lender. These limits help minimize credit risks by diversifying a lender's limited resources across borrowers and over time. Practitioners should also advise a microenterprise lender to establish a written policy regarding loan interest rates. These should give due consideration to restrictions established by its investors, the nonprofit nature of the microenterprise lender, and all applicable federal and state laws.
- *Collateral*: If a borrower has collateral and the microenterprise lender takes a security interest in collateral, the lender should be aware of the filing requirements for perfecting that security interest. States have additional filing requirements for specific types of property such as a motor vehicle.
- *Default*: Lawyers can assist microenterprise practitioners in determining events of default that strike a balance between protecting the interest and integrity of the microenterprise lender and providing low-income borrowers with the time and flexibility to establish successful businesses (including opportunities to cure defaults).
- *State and Federal Laws:* Lawyers can also help microenterprise practitioners understand the applicability of state and federal banking laws and/or lending laws and other federal statutes such as the Truth in Lending Act and the Equal Credit Opportunity Act.

I. Collection Practices

Microenterprise programs must decide how they will handle collection matters for loan installments that are not made on time. A significant goal of microenterprise programs is the development of business acumen. Thus, programs must determine whether a flexible or static approach to loan repayment will best facilitate this acumen. Reserve accounts or "rainy day" accounts, discussed below in Section L, are sometimes required as an alternate payment source in the event of an emergency. Otherwise, collection is the only option. As noted in Section H, above, federal and state laws dictate acceptable collection practices.

J. Borrower Bankruptcy

Any new business may fail. As most microentrepreneurs do not have a lot of money, the chance that their business could fail may be even greater. How, then, can a microenterprise program protect itself from the bankruptcy of a microloan borrower?

One way is to ask for a personal guarantee from the individual owners (and sometimes even their spouses) if the business is organized as a corporation or limited liability company (LLC). With a personal guarantee, if the corporation or the LLC goes bankrupt, the lender can still recover from the person guaranteeing the loan. However, the individual borrower can be sued (sometimes in small claims court if the amount of the loan is very small, usually $1,000–$7,500). If a judgment is obtained, wages can be garnished and bank accounts can be attached. Some jurisdictions require corporations (even nonprofits) to be represented by counsel.[30]

Another way to protect against borrower bankruptcy is to have the borrower pledge a personal asset, such as a house. Because many borrowers who are seeking microloans do not have collateral, this approach may not be effective. Based on experience, many microenterprise programs find that there are two realistic solutions: (1) taking a security interest in goods purchased with the loan money or (2) doing a loan "work out" which, in the case of a pre-bankrupt business, may involve

30. D.C. Super. Ct. R.—Small Claims 9 (2004).

trying to save the business by recommending business consultants or ultimately refinancing the loan on terms that are easier for the borrower.

Microenterprise lenders and microbusinesses alike may find some information about U.S. bankruptcy laws useful. The law of bankruptcy is based on the U.S. Bankruptcy Code and is divided into different chapters. The federal court system handles bankruptcy. Though an individual can be forced into bankruptcy, it is usually voluntary. Microloan borrowers organized as sole proprietorships, partnerships, corporations, or limited liability companies may file Chapter 7 for an orderly liquidation. Alternatively, business entities may be reorganized under Chapter 11. Although businesses are not generally able to file under Chapter 13, a sole proprietor may be able to file as an individual and include business debts for which he or she is personally liable.

K. Dispute Resolution Mechanisms for Borrowers and Lenders

The loan agreement between the borrower and the lender should indicate what will happen if the borrower defaults on the loan or if the lender fails to live up to its obligations under the contract. Generally, the lender has the option of suing the borrower (in small claims court if the loan is under a certain amount), mediating, or arbitrating the dispute. Because a central part of a microenterprise program should be to encourage self-sufficiency for borrowers, alternative dispute resolution mechanisms such as mediation or arbitration should be encouraged whenever possible before commencing litigation.[31] In addition, because arbitration can be expensive, mediation or small claims court may be the most expeditious ways to proceed.

L. Banking Issues for Microenterprise Programs

Some microenterprise programs require participants to have a forced savings or "rainy day account." Participants must contribute money to

31. Sometimes there is a legitimate reason for default, such as a death in the family, and there is an easy way to negotiate a solution, such as lowering the borrower's payments for a few months.

this account periodically—for example, every two weeks.[32] In the event a microentrepreneur cannot afford to make a loan payment, the amount would be taken from this forced savings account to avoid default. In addition, it ensures that there is a back-up repayment source in the event the borrower does not pay an installment. The account may also serve as collateral for the loans.

As a general rule, state and federal banking laws will not apply to a microenterprise lender unless it has voluntarily chartered itself as a state or federal banking entity or if it accepts deposits. A local banking institution may be willing to lend its support to the microenterprise program by waiving fees for accounts opened by the self-employment associations.(See also Chapter 4.B.)

Lawyers representing microenterprise programs and microbusinesses should be aware of another banking issue—the emergence of Individual Development Accounts (IDAs). Similar to Individual Retirement Accounts (IRAs), IDAs are based on the premise that people escape poverty and achieve wealth though asset accumulation, not simply income. These restricted accounts are set up in the name of an individual, initiated as early as birth, and are restricted to high-return investments such as college education, starting a small business, or buying a first home.[33]

---

32. One adaptation of the Grameen Bank peer-lending model is the maintenance of individual rather than group savings accounts. *See* Counts, *supra* note 2, at xviii.

33. For more information about IDAs see MICHAEL SHERRADEN, ASSETS AND THE POOR: A NEW AMERICAN WELFARE POLICY (1991), Robert Friedman, *Individual Development Accounts: From Local Experiment to National Impact*, CORP. FOR ENTERPRISE DEV. 1996 ENTREPRENEURIAL ECON. REV. 16, 16, and materials from the First International Conference on Individual Development Accounts, held Nov. 13–15, 1995 (on file with the Center for Social Development, the Corporation for Enterprise Development, and the author). You can also visit the Corporation for Enterprise Development Website at www.cfed.org. The Corporation for Enterprise Development (CFED) fosters widely shared and sustainable economic well-being. CFED promotes asset-building and economic opportunity strategies, primarily in low-income and distressed communities, that bring together community practice, public policy, and private markets in new and effective ways.

CHAPTER **4**

Planning Issues for Microenterprise Programs

Lawyers can also be helpful in addressing the many planning concerns of microenterprise development programs.

A. Analyzing Community Resources and Target Populations

Some microenterprise programs target a particular population, such as women who are trying to get off welfare, victims of domestic violence, Native Americans, dislocated workers, or immigrants. Each of these populations has a unique set of needs. For this reason, it is important to analyze community resources for assisting a target population. For example, the U.S. Department of Health and Human Services, Office of Refugee Resettlement, provides programs and assistance for refugees.

Groups interested in beginning a microenterprise program should assess the needs of the community and review other programs servicing the area. Microenterprise programs compete with a variety of financial concerns, from finance companies to federal and local disaster relief programs. Therefore, in order to ensure that groups do not duplicate the efforts of similar programs in the community, it is essential that they do a considerable amount of research and planning before instituting a microenterprise program. In addition, groups must think seriously about commitment and be prepared for the long haul because microenterprises are expensive to operate and involve a large time commitment for practitioners. In fact, microenterprise programs entail much more than loaning money; microenterprise program staff will be involved in a wide range of activities from coordinating volunteers to loan collections in the community. Further, programs likely will find that technical assistance needs will take a great deal of time and resources even if the program does not intend to make technical assistance and training a primary task. Perhaps most important, programs take on a serious moral commitment to their clients.

B. Legal and Business Issues for Peer Lending Groups

Peer lending is also known as circle lending or group lending. Because this model comes from the Grameen ("Village") Bank in Bangladesh and other programs like it in the developing world, it is sometimes referred to as village banking.[1] Group lending is a methodology for credit delivery which is intended to mitigate the risks of lending to a borrower with no collateral.[2] It involves forming groups who may guarantee each other's loans and help each other's businesses. This peer pressure boosts repayment. Group members are expected to keep their loans current or members of the group will not be able to receive further loans. These borrowing groups are sometimes called self-employment associations, and they may encounter a host of legal issues, such as:

- How will the group govern itself?
- Does it have bylaws?
- How will it allocate loans to members of the group?
- Will it engage in other businesses as a group?
- Will the group itself make loans to its members?
- What happens if a member of the group becomes disabled?
- What is the group process for collecting from a defaulting member?
- Does the group have a tax identification number to open a bank account?

---

1. *See* David Burnstein, *The Barefoot Bank with Cheek*, ATLANTIC MONTHLY, Dec. 1995, at 40.
2. *See* 2002 Directory, *supra* note 5, at xiii.

The answers to these and other legal questions depend on the relevant state statutes and the intricacies of the lending model. For example, self-employment associations may be legally organized as partnerships (per the terms of a written partnership agreement) or as an unincorporated association (taxed as a partnership) governed by written bylaws[3] or as limited liability companies.

Example

Dorothy Wallace seemed like a lender's nightmare. Separated from her husband, she and her two teenagers were on welfare. She hadn't held a steady job since 1984 and had made mistakes that ruined her credit rating. With an $800 loan from the Chicago-based Women's Self Employment Project (WSEP), Ms. Wallace increased her inventory of additive-free lotion, cologne, and perfume that she was selling to steady customers in downtown offices and other locations.

WSEP was founded in 1986 to assist low-income women interested in self-employment as a way out of poverty. Although Ms. Wallace was grateful for the money, she was especially grateful for the moral support that WSEP provided. "They gave me a chance to start all over again . . . ." This support explains why she and the four other women in her borrowing circle were so diligent about making their payments.

One member of the circle was able to sell jewelry that she made after borrowing $600 for materials. Another was a retired bank clerk who sold hand-sewn lingerie and linens; she borrowed $700 to buy a heavy-duty sewing machine. A former Head Start aide, who borrowed $500, sold custom gift baskets and peddled fruit on street corners and in parks as a member of the circle. A woman with four children of her own and four foster children hoped to learn to read and to get a day care license because of the circle. Wallace and the other women in her borrowing circle named it "Too Blessed."

The Too Blessed circle operated just like all the others that WSEP has established. The five members first chose two members to re-

3. Distinguishable from a "pure" peer-lending model, where all members of the borrowing group are obligated on the loan, is the individual lending model. In this instance the loan is made to an individual, not to a group, and the legal issues are much less complex. The individual lending model generally requires some form of collateral.

ceive loans. The first two borrowers had to keep their loans current for six weeks. In addition, all five members of the circle had to attend three meetings in a row before a third member was eligible for loan money. This element of peer pressure helped ensure timely repayment.[4]

C. Planning Tips

Microenterprise practitioners have identified other issues that microenterprise programs should consider.

- *Flexibility*: Programs should maintain flexibility over loan funds. If loan funds are too restricted, the program may have difficulty making loans and getting the money into the hands of worthy borrowers. Some practitioners view federal funds as being more restrictive but there are exceptions such as the U.S. Small Business Administration's Microloan Program. Negotiating "string free funds" from lenders is an important way to maintain flexibility so that microenterprise funds can cover administrative costs.
- *Operating costs:* Funding operating costs can be a major challenge for microenterprise programs. Buying a computer and hiring a collection agency are examples of important operating tools. A smaller microenterprise program may be able to use a home-based small business accounting system.
- *Competition:* Programs should examine the competition and the client base when determining what interest rate to offer borrowers. The competition will often be high-interest lenders as opposed to commercial banks. Microloans are generally offered at market rate because their goal is to provide access to capital, not charity.
- *Interest rates:* It is possible to negotiate interest rates with microenterprise program lenders. Typical interest rates range from several points above the prime rate to rates of 12% or 13%.
- *Multiple loans:* If the microenterprise program is managing a number of loans, it should make sure that its interest rate is consistent

4. David Wessell, *Doing Business in the Inner City—Small Victories: Two Unusual Lenders Show How 'Bad Risks' Can Be Good Business*, WALL ST. J., June 23, 1992, at A1.

with each type of loan. Matching borrowers to a particular funding source takes additional time and work.

- *Reporting*: If a bank services the microloans, it is important for the bank and the microenterprise program staff to maintain close communication. Negotiate with the bank for timely reports on borrowers' payments. These reports should be weekly or bi-weekly; monthly reports are insufficient because they allow for extended unsupervised periods of default. The microenterprise programs need to know immediately if borrowers are having trouble making loan payments.

D. Working with Target Populations

1. Temporary Assistance for Needy Families (the Aftermath of Welfare Reform)

Since their inception in the United States, microenterprise development organizations have targeted welfare recipients. Researchers continue to examine microenterprise as a welfare-to-work strategy. For example, the Charles Stewart Mott Foundation initiated a Microenterprise Welfare-to-Work Demonstration and Evaluation in 1998.[5] Working in collaboration with the Microenterprise Fund for Innovation, Effectiveness, Learning and Dissemination (FIELD) of the Aspen Institute[6] and the

5. NISHA PATEL AND MARK GREENBERG, CENTER FOR LAW AND SOCIAL POLICY, MICROENTERPRISE DEVELOPMENT AND SELF-EMPLOYMENT FOR TANF RECIPIENTS: STATE EXPERIENCES AND ISSUES IN TANF REAUTHORIZATION (2002), *available at* www.clasp.org/DMS/Documents/1023820695.1/microenterprise_report.pdf. *See also* Pamela Friedman, *Microenterprise Development: An Employment Option for Welfare Recipients*, Vol 5, No. 2 WELFARE INFORMATION NETWORK, ISSUE NOTES (January 2001); MARK GREENBERG, DEVELOPING POLICIES TO SUPPORT MICROENTERPRISE IN THE TANF STRUCTURE: A GUIDE TO THE LAW, *available at* www.fieldus.org/li/pdf/clasp.pdf; Lisa Servon and Timothy Bates, *Microenterprise as an Exit Route from Poverty: Recommendations for Programs and Policy Makers*, 20 J. OF URBAN AFFAIRS 419 (1998); Lisa Servon, *From Public Assistance to Self-Sufficiency: The Role for the Microenterprise Strategy*, COMMUNITIES AND BANKING (Fed. Reserve Bank of Boston 1999), *available at* www.bos.frb.org/commdev/pdf/spring99.pdf; AMY KAYS BLAIR AND JOYCE KLEIN, MICROENTERPRISE AS A WELFARE TO WORK STRATEGY: CLIENT CHARACTERISTICS, MICROENTERPRISE FUND FOR INNOVATION, EFFECTIVENESS, LEARNING AND DISSEMINATION (FIELD) OF THE ASPEN INSTITUTE (July 2001), *available at* www.fieldus.org/publications/WTWResearch%20Report1.pdf.

6. Headquartered in Washington, D.C., the Aspen Institute is an international non-profit organization founded in 1950. Its mission is to foster enlightened leadership, the appreciation of timeless ideas and values, and open-minded dialogue on contemporary issues. Through seminars, policy programs, conferences and leadership development initiatives, the Institute and its inter-

Center for Law and Social Policy (CLASP)[7] the purpose of the project is to determine under what circumstances self-employment could be a route to economic self-sufficiency for recipients of Temporary Assistance for Needy Families (TANF).[8]

The Personal Responsibility and Work Opportunity Reconciliation Act of 1996[9] (PRWORA) dramatically overhauled a 61-year-old federal guarantee of cash assistance to the nation's poorest children and replaced it with lump-sum federal grants that states must use within certain parameters.[10] Most notably, the law prohibits states from using federal block grant funds to assist a family for more than five years, subject to limited exceptions, and requires adults to be "engaged in work" within two years of receiving assistance, or sooner at the state's option. The law also cut food stamps and restricted forms of social services and public assistance for most legal immigrants during their first five years in the United States.[11]

Earlier laws such as Aid to Families with Dependent Children (AFDC), which provided income support to families with children deprived of parental support, Job Opportunities and Basic Skills Training (JOBS), which created employment and training programs for AFDC recipients, and Emergency Assistance (EA), which provided short-term emergency services and benefits to needy families have now been replaced by TANF.[12]

---

national partners seek to promote the pursuit of common ground and deeper understanding in a nonpartisan and non-ideological setting. *See* www.aspeninstitute.org. (last visited Feb. 6, 2004). Created in 1998, FIELD is a program of the Aspen Institute. FIELD's mission is to identify, develop and disseminate the best practices in microenterprise development, and to broadly educate policymakers, funders and others about microenterprise as an antipoverty intervention. *See* www.fieldus.org (last visited Feb. 6, 2004).

7. *See supra* note 23.

8. *See* Microenterprise as a Welfare to Work Strategy: Two Year Findings, The Aspen Institute FIELD (2002), *available at* www.fieldus.org/publications/WTWRpt3.pdf (last visited Feb. 13, 2004) for preliminary findings. The microenterprise organizations that participated in the demonstration and learning assessment represented various regions and included: Detroit Entrepreneurship Institute (DEI), Detroit, Michigan; Institute for Social and Economic Development (ISED), Iowa City, Iowa; Little Sisters of the Assumption Family Health Services (Project Hope), Dorchester, Massachusetts; MiCasa Resource Center for Women, Denver, Colorado; Southern Oregon Women's Access to Credit, Inc, Medford, Oregon; West Company, Ukiah, California; Women's Initiative for Self-Employment (WI), San Francisco, California; Women's Self Employment Project (WESP), Chicago, Illinois; Women Venture (WV), St. Paul, Minnesota; and Worker Ownership Resource Center (WORC), Geneva, New York.

9. Pub. L. No. 104-193, 110 Stat. 2105 (1996).

10. *See* PRWORA § 103, 110 Stat. at 2137.

11. For more information on immigrants and specific social services, consult Matthew Bender, Immigration Law and Procedure.

12. Other public benefits include: (1) Supplemental Security Income (SSI), (2) Medicaid, and (3) federal and state housing subsidies that are dependent on income. Eligibility for these programs

Under the TANF Block Grant each state had to begin a program of assistance to needy families no later than July 1, 1997. In order to receive a TANF grant, a state must submit a state plan to the U.S. Department of Health and Human Services (HHS).[13]

Once the plan is submitted, HHS then determines whether the plan contains the information required by law. Generally, state block grants are set to reflect the amount of federal funds that the state was receiving during the early 1990s under the set of programs that were repealed at the time TANF was enacted.[14] States must satisfy a basic maintenance of effort (MOE) which requires states to spend 75 to 80% of their historic state expenditures for "qualified expenditures" in cash assistance, child care assistance, and educational activities to facilitate increased self-sufficiency, job training, work related administrative costs reasonably calculated to accomplish the purposes of TANF and other expenditures.[15] The state may choose whether to spend its MOE dollars in its TANF program, or in one or more separate state programs.[16]

It is important to note that under PRWORA there are now no federally mandated asset limits and income exclusions. Before, the old AFDC rules penalized microentrepreneurs on welfare; loans of $1,000 or more would disqualify a person from receiving welfare because loans or any saving or working capital could not be accumulated for the business since the loan is an asset that reduces eligibility for benefits. Thus, the old welfare structure did not distinguish personal assets from

---

is based on financial need. Another category of public benefits is insurance based. Examples of insurance-based public benefits are Social Security and unemployment. Laws regarding these benefits may also impact microentrepreneurs. SSI is a welfare-based program that must be distinguished from Social Security Retirement (or Social Security), which is based on a history of employment and contributions into the system. A person may receive SSI if he is financially eligible and fits into one of the following categories: (1) over 65 years old; (2) blind; or (3) disabled. A person receiving Social Security may still qualify for SSI if he is categorically eligible (*e.g.*, aged, blind, or disabled) and meets financial eligibility standards. Generally, a person is not eligible for SSI if she has more than $2,000 in resources. The resource limit for a couple is $3,000. *See* 20 C.F.R. § 416.1201(a)(2000). Medicaid is a federal-state health insurance program that is based on need and eligibility. Under the old AFDC system, recipients were automatically entitled to receive Medicaid, which covers most medical expenses including prescriptions and long-term care. Housing subsidies and public housing exist at the federal and state level including the U.S. Department of Housing and Urban Development (HUD) Section 8 program and other housing benefits determined by individual and household income. Another public service includes the food stamp program, which is federally administered by the U.S. Department of Agriculture (USDA). Food stamps benefits are made available to low income individuals and households through the state or local social service agency.

13. *See* PRWORA § 103, 110 Stat. at 2113.

14. *See id.* at 2113-17.

15. PRWORA § 103, 110 Stat. at 2124.

16. *Id.*

cash obtained through business loans or the value of capital equipment, nor did it allow welfare recipients to deduct the repayment of the loan principal as a business expense.[17]

In the present regime, each of the 50 states determines asset and income exclusions for microenterprise borrowers.[18] Asset rules or restrictions may still exist for eligibility for other services such as public housing and food stamps.[19] Under TANF, each state will determine the obstacles to and incentives for self-employment. It is estimated that 5 to 10% of welfare recipients may be able to benefit from self-employment.[20] Approximately 40 million people used public assistance programs during each month in 1995.[21]

As this section demonstrates, TANF is a complex maze and lawyers working with microenterprise development organizations play a key role in interpreting the law.

---

17. *See* David E. Anderson, *Report Urges Microenterprise as Step Away from Welfare,* UPI, June 27, 1991, available in LEXISNexis Library, UPI File; *Bill Would Allow Welfare and Small Business Loan,* GANNETT NEWS SERVICE, June 28, 1991 (available in LEXIS, Nexis, GNS File); Constance L. Hays, *Girl's Plan to Save for College Runs Afoul of Welfare Rules,* N.Y. TIMES, May 15, 1992, at A1 (describing the AFDC asset rules which required a young woman whose family received AFDC to spend $4,900 that she had saved for college to ensure her family's continued eligibility for AFDC); William Raspberry, *Why Shackle Poor who Want to Start Businesses,* ATLANTA J. & CONST., July 2, 1991, at A7.

In order to allow self-employed welfare recipients to keep their AFDC benefits during the first year after self-employment and to allow them to accumulate income and assets for their businesses, waivers for the federal rules had to be obtained. Initially, the federal government approved five pilot programs to test the viability of microenterprise groups. These test programs, run by the Self-Employment Investment Demonstration, were in Michigan, Minnesota, Iowa, Mississippi and Maryland. *See* CYNTHIA A. GUY, ET AL., MANPOWER DEMONSTRATION RESEARCH GROUP, SELF-EMPLOYMENT FOR WELFARE RECIPIENTS: IMPLEMENTATION OF THE SEID PROGRAM vii, 17-18 (1991).

Under section 1115 of the Social Security Act, the Secretary of HHS may approve research and demonstration project proposals. This section authorizes experimental, pilot or demonstration project proposals that promote innovative improvements in the administration and execution of public assistance and related services or help recipients of public assistance and related services to reduce their dependency. Waivers are still available under TANF, but as a practical matter, have far less relevance under TANF, for two reasons: states have broader discretion in use of TANF funds; and states can only receive waivers of TANF state plan requirements, and the principal TANF restrictions do not appear in the state plan provisions of the law.

18. *See* RAY BOSHARA ET AL., CORPORATION FOR ENTERPRISE DEVELOPMENT, REALIZING THE PROMISE OF MICROENTERPRISE DEVELOPMENT IN WELFARE REFORM 30 (1997) [hereinafter Realizing].

19. *See* Margaret Beebe Held, *Developing Microbusinesses in Public Housing: Notes from the Field,* 31 HARV. C.R.-C.L. L. REV. 473, 481–90 (1996) (describing local public housing authority obstacles and possibilities for locating microbusinesses in public housing).

20. *See* Rona F. Feit & Sheela Rani Das, *Wading Through Waivers: Enabling Self-Employment for Welfare Entrepreneurs,* CORP. FOR ENTERPRISE DEV. 1990 ENTREPRENEURIAL ECON. REV. at 3.

21. *See* Jan Tin, Bureau of the Census, U.S. Dept. of Com., Pub. No. P70-79, Dynamics of Economic Well-Being: Program Participation, 1993-1995, Who Gets Assistance (2001).

Lawyers representing microenterprise programs should be aware of several points. First, use of TANF dollars to support microenterprise training and practitioners is an allowable use of TANF funds. Second, to avoid a TANF penalty, each state faces steadily escalating "participation rates." Only certain activities are countable toward these rates. As a result, a state may be hesitant to allow involvement in microenterprise activities unless the state is confident that allowing such activities will not put the state at risk of failing to meet the required participation rate.[22]

Although supporters of microenterprise development believe there is no "right way" to structure state spending and that states should implement creative ideas, the third model of separating TANF from state funds may be preferable as a means of helping microentrepreneurs without subjecting them to TANF time limits and prescriptive work requirements.[23] Moreover, states can develop new alternatives to welfare and policies can be created that are not "welfare specific."

Lawyers can also play a significant role in lobbying their state to include microenterprise development as part of a state plan. Because key decisions are left to states under TANF, a state is free to reconsider its policies at any time, and if initial policies were not supportive of microenterprise, a state can revisit those policies. To this end, microenterprise advocates have carefully identified 14 significant recommendations that are important to maximizing the success of microenterprise development:

1. States should recognize microenterprise development as a legitimate welfare-to-work strategy.
2. States should attempt to offer microenterprise opportunities to welfare recipients that will not count against state or federal time limits on assistance, due to the high risks and high rewards of microenterprise development.
3. States should pursue loan capital, seed capital, and IDAs from outside the welfare system such as the Small Business Administration and community development financial institutions.

22. *See* Mark Greenberg, Developing Policies to Support Microenterprise in the TANF Structure: A Guide to the Law, *supra* note 1; Nisha Patel and Mark Greenberg, *supra* note 1.

23. *Id.*

4. To the extent that microenterprise development is pursued within TANF, microenterprise should be defined as vocational educational training; once the business has been started, the self-employment should be classified as unsubsidized employment.
5. States should increase earned income disregards, including allowing disregards of business income, in order to increase work and reduce reliance on assistance.
6. Regarding the treatment of assets and income, states should set reasonable auto, business, IDA, and personal asset limits, as well as ensure the protection of home ownership for all recipients. At a minimum, $8,000 in business assets, $2,000 in personal assets, and $10,000 in an IDA should be allowed.
7. Only business income actually drawn from the business for personal use should be considered by the state in determining monthly levels of assistance.
8. States should ensure access to health insurance programs or Medicaid that are not tied to an income support system.
9. States should provide childcare training for participants and for a specified period of time consider providing child-care subsidies for business start-ups.
10. Following the Illinois example, states should fund assistance for working families with state rather than federal dollars so that months of such assistance will not count against the five-year federal time limit.
11. A minimum of six months of training and two years of business operations should be allowed for welfare recipients to develop viable businesses.
12. States should consider the development of a stipend for microenterprise development outside of the welfare system or alternatively, dedicate a percentage of MOE funds to microenterprise if the state has a commingled (financial assistance from federal and state sources) system.
13. Microenterprise programs should be framed broadly and integrated with other job creation, skill building, education and workforce development strategies.
14. Microenterprise programs should be developed as employment and training programs for welfare recipients who expect the micro-business to be a major source of income and they should be developed in partnership with programs so that they are available to

entrepreneurs as "income patching" (e.g., to supplement low-wage jobs).[24]

Current research on microenterprise and TANF has resulted in additional recommendations that would lend support to microenterprise development and self-employment. These include:

1. sustaining federal TANF and state MOE funding levels with inflation adjustments;
2. enacting a wage supplement proposal disregarding months on TANF while recipients are employed (and self-employed) in calculating the total months on the five-year federal time limit;
3. increasing child care funding to improve the quality of care and the availability of child care;
4. mandating that states describe in their child care plans and annual reports, efforts to strengthen the affordability, accessibility and continuity of child care;
5. providing federal funding for research on barriers affecting families' access to child care and surveys of child care providers to identify ways to improve access to quality, affordable child care and provider participation;
6. extending Transitional Medical Assistance beyond 12 months;
7. making poverty reduction an explicit goal of TANF; and
8. providing incentives for states to emphasize improving employment outcomes for people who leave TANF.[25]

Example

After her marriage deteriorated, 23-year-old Sally Jones needed welfare and food stamps to support herself and her two children. She recounts her story:[26]

It was very hard. I went to the food stamp office and they told me to fill out forms or else I wouldn't get the benefits. Even though I

24. *See* Realizing, *supra* note 18 at 32–37, Realizing the Promise of Microenterprise Development at www.CLASP.org (last visited Feb. 6, 2004).

25. *See* Mark Greenberg, Developing Policies to Support Microenterprise in the TANF Structure: A Guide to the Law, *supra* note 1; Nisha Patel and Mark Greenberg, *supra*, note 1; *see also* www.clasp.org (last visited June 30, 2004) for more information on TANF reauthorization.

26. This story is a true account of one microbusiness owner's experience. For privacy, her identity has not been disclosed.

had a high school diploma, I had a third grade reading level and couldn't fill out the forms. When I went to apply for jobs, they gave me an application to fill out. No one thought to ask me if I could read. The applications were like Greek to me. I realized that I would need help reading in order to get a job and feed my children so I went to the local library and asked if someone there could teach me to read.

Through a local microenterprise program I learned about how I could start my own business. Twenty people showed up for the first class. I had experience cleaning houses for $25 a day so I thought, why not start my own business doing that. In my work with the literacy program my reading level increased from the third grade to the eighth grade. I haven't been on welfare in six years. I can read to my kids and we read the Bible everyday. I can now earn $200 a day. I make $48,000 a year and my goal is to make $60,000. I don't panic anymore. I feel great. I have confidence in myself.

2. Immigrants and Refugees

Self-employment is the only option for many immigrants and refugees. Accordingly, some microenterprise development organizations target these populations.[27] The Office of Refugee Resettlement (ORR) in the U.S. Department of Health and Human Services oversees refugee resettlement and it is responsible for employment, training, and placement of refugees so that they can achieve economic self-sufficiency as quickly as possible.[28] The ORR Refugee Microenterprise Program was created to enable refugees to increase household income and decrease the likelihood of relying on public assistance.[29] Other Federal programs such as the Program for Investment in Microentrepreneurs (PRIME) have also helped to fund business development programs for refugee-owned microbusinesses and others.[30]

27. John F. Else and Carmel Clay Thompson, Refugee Microenterprise Development: Achievements and Lessons Learned, April 1998, *available at* www.ised.org/research&evaluation/documents/Refugee%20ME%20lessons%20learned.pdf (last visited Feb. 6, 2004) (analyzing the experience and achievements to 16 refugee microenterprise programs funded by the ORR from 1991–1996).

28. *Id.*

29. *Id.*

30. Anne Gonzalez, *Microloan Gives Boost to Immigrants*, Sacramento Business Journal, *available at* www.sacramento.bizjournals.com/sacramento/stories/2002/02/04/smallb1.html (last visited Feb. 6, 2004).

According to ORR statistics, since 1975, approximately 2.4 million refugees have been resettled in the United States. In 2001, 84,000 refugees, entrants, and Amerasians were admitted to the U.S. for resettlement.[31] Under the U.S. Immigration and Nationality Act (INA),[32] to qualify as a refugee a person must have a well-founded fear of persecution in their country of origin because of their race, religion, nationality, membership in a particular social group, or political opinion.[33] The INA allows refugees who have been so classified while outside the United States to be admitted to the United States on a humanitarian basis. Priority is afforded to refugees with special ties to the United States, such as former U.S. Government employees, employees of a U.S. company, persons with close relatives living in the United States, and/or persons whose persecution is specifically related to an individual's association with the U.S. Government.[34]

Also, asylum applicants who have been granted legal status as asylees[35] are eligible for refugee benefits and services as of the date that they are granted asylum.[36]

The INA broadly defines an immigrant as "any alien in the United States, except one legally admitted under specific nonimmigrant categories."[37] The terms immigrant and lawful permanent resident may also be used interchangeably and refer to persons who hold "green cards." Under the INA, lawful permanent residents are legally accorded the privilege of residing permanently in the United States after either being issued immigrant visas by the U.S. Department of State overseas or adjusted to permanent resident status by the United States Citizenship and Immigration Services (USCIS) within the Department of Home-

31. See Office of Refugee Resettlement Website at www.acf.hhs.gov/programs/orr/mission/factsheet.htm. (last visited Jan. 30, 2004).

32. 8 U.S.C. § 1101 *et seq.* (2000).

33. 8 U.S.C. § 1153 (2000).

34. *Id.*

35. An "asylee" is defined as an alien "in the United States or at a port of entry who is found to be unable or unwilling to return to his or her country of nationality, or to seek the protection of that country because of persecution or a well-founded fear of persecution. Persecution or the fear thereof must be based on the alien's race, religion, nationality, membership in a particular social group, or political opinion. For persons with no nationality, the country of nationality is considered to be the country in which the alien last habitually resided. Asylees are eligible to adjust to lawful permanent resident status after one year of continuous presence in the United States. These immigrants are limited to 10,000 adjustments per fiscal year." *See* www.uscis.gov/graphics/glossary.htm (last visited Feb. 13, 2004).

36. *See also* Office of Refugee Resettlement Website *at* www.acf.hhs.gov/programs/orr/mission/factsheet.htm (last visited Jan. 30, 2004).

37. 8 U.S.C. § 1101(a)(15) (2000).

land Security (the agency that replaced the U.S. Immigration and Naturalization Service after the terrorist attacks of September 11, 2001).[38]

Lawyers working with microenterprise development organizations and microbusinesses must be aware that there may be immigration consequences for microentrepreneurs who are not lawful permanent residents (green card holders) or who do not otherwise have legal authorization to work. While this is a complex area of law, the following information will give microenterprise staff and their legal counsel basic information on how self-employment is viewed under the INA and by the USCIS. Competent immigration counsel should be consulted to avoid adverse consequences.

The word "employment" is not defined in the Immigration and Nationality Act.[39] The only definition of employment is in the employment sanction regulations at 8 C.F.R. § 274a (Control of Employment of Aliens), which states that "[t]he term 'employment' means any service or labor performed by an employee for an employer within the United States . . . . However, employment does not include casual employment by individuals who provide domestic service in a private home that is sporadic, irregular or intermittent."[40]

These regulations refer to services provided for wages or other compensation and exclude independent contractors or casual domestic service. These limitations are relevant to the enforcement of employer sanctions that are penalties for employers who knowingly hire aliens unauthorized to work by the USCIS.

What constitutes employment remains unclear in some contexts. For the purposes of eligibility for adjustment of status (applying for permanent residence in the United States without having to leave this country), unauthorized employment may not include voluntary services without pay, work engaged in to acquire experience, self-employment in a one-person business, and an employee's leave without pay.[41]

If the microenterprise participant is a bona-fide non-immigrant in certain categories, such as a student or a visitor, self-employment may be a bar to change of status from that non-immigrant visa category to another.[42] Other non-immigrant visa classifications, such as foreign em-

38. On November 25, 2002 the President signed the Homeland Security Act of 2002 into law, transferring Immigration and Naturalization Service functions to the new Department of Homeland Security.

39. *See* 8 U.S.C. §§ 1101-1503; 18 U.S.C. §§ 1114, 1429, 1546; 22 U.S.C. §§ 618, 1446 (2000).

40. *Id.*

41. *See generally* Bender, Matthew, Immigration Law and Procedure (rev'd ed. 2004).

42. *See In re Tong,* 16 I & N Dec. 593, 593 (BIA 1978): *see also In re Minei,* 11 I & N Dec. 430, 430 (Reg. Comm'r) (applicant made ineligible for change of status to B-1 business visitor due to his self-employment as a performer).

bassy employees (A-1) or temporary workers or trainees (H-1 or H-2), have inherent employment authorization to work only for a specific employer. Other immigration classifications, such as asylee or refugee, allow for employment as part of that status. Some other non-immigrants, such as students, must apply for work authorization. In some immigration contexts, even non-salaried work may be deemed employment.[43]

Furthermore, microenterprise participants who hire employees must comply with Employer Sanction Laws, which require employers to document that employees are eligible to work in the United States.[44] In addition, some microenterprise practitioners who work with refugees and whose programs are funded by ORS have reported that many refugees apply for citizenship in order to be eligible for services such as food stamps and welfare that are no longer available to refugees under PRWORA. Refugees who become citizens are no longer eligible for ORS funding; services for these clients must be secured from other sources.[45]

In short, legal advice should be obtained when working with microentrepreneurs who are not immigrants or refugees.[46]

Example

New York Lawyers for the Public Interest (NYLPI), a nonprofit law office that operates a pro bono clearinghouse to provide free legal assistance for eligible low income individuals and community

43. *See Tong,* 16 I & N Dec. at 593; *Minei,* 11 I & N Dec. at 430.

44. *See* Immigration Reform and Control Act (IRCA) of 1986, 7 U.S.C. § 2025; 8 U.S.C. §§ 1101, 1152, 1153, 1160, 1161, 1184, 1186, 1187, 1252, 1254, 1255, 1255a, 1258, 1259, 1321, 1324, 1324a, 1324b, 1357, 1364, 1365; 18 U.S.C. § 1546; 20 U.S.C. §§ 1091, 1096; 29 U.S.C. §§ 1802, 1813, 1816, 1851; 42 U.S.C. §§ 303, 405, 502, 602, 603, 672, 673, 1203, 1320b-7, 1353, 1383, 1396b, 1436a, 1437r (1986); 8 C.F.R. § 274a (1997) (Control of Employment of Aliens).

45. A refugee must be a lawful permanent resident (LPR) for five years before he or she is eligible to apply for citizenship and in many instances the administrative delay after an LPR applies for naturalization with the INS can be one year or more. Lawyers can play a significant role in lobbying efforts for changes in administrative agency rules and regulations which impact microenterprise development. In this instance it is arguable that there should be a period of transition when a microentrepreneur ceases to be a refugee to become a naturalized United States citizen.

46. The American Immigration Lawyers Association, 1400 I Street, N.W., Washington, D.C. (202) 371-9377; www.aila.org) has a directory of member lawyers. There are immigration law legal clinics at the following law schools: University of Arizona, Boston University, Brigham Young, Brooklyn, City University of New York (CUNY) at Queens College, The George Washington University Law School, Loyola University of New Orleans Law School, New York Law School, Notre Dame, Seattle, Seton Hall, St. Mary's University of San Antonio, St. Thomas University, Touro, Tulane, University of California at Berkeley Boalt Hall, University of California at Davis, University of California at Hastings, University of Minnesota, University of San Diego, University of Washington, Widener, and Yale. There are also a number of immigration social service agencies that can help. These listings can be obtained from the local telephone directory.

groups, brokered the relationship between a microenterprise development program and a law firm. Over several years more that 15 attorneys from Debevoite and Plimpton worked with the New York Association for New Americans (NYANA) Microenterprise Development Program which helps immigrant and refugee entrepreneurs learn about the American marketplace and how to apply for a loan to start a business. The law firm has drafted lending documents for NYANA, America's largest not-for-profit provider of educational social, legal and business services to refugees and immigrants. The firm's assistance to microbusinesses has included workshops on legal compliance and technical assistance to individual entrepreneurs as well as assisting with a landlord and tenant dispute and representing a microentrepreneur in the purchase of a fast food business.[47]

3. Domestic Violence Survivors

The microenterprise industry is working with domestic violence advocates to enhance opportunities for domestic violence survivors interested in entrepreneurship. National studies show that approximately 22 to 25% of women are physically abused at some point in their lives.[48] A growing number of microenterprise organizations are working with domestic violence survivors.

For example, the Wyoming Coalition Again Domestic Violence and Sexual Assault began work in microenterprise development in 1999 to create viable options for women's economic development. The Coalition formed the Wyoming Women's Business Center, which serves domestic violence survivors and others interested in microbusiness. Proponents of collaboration between the domestic violence activists and the microenterprise community observe that entrepreneurship is an important option for domestic violence survivors because they have often been prevented from sustaining employment at meaningful wages. Indeed, the abuse often includes deliberate interference with the woman's employment and education, as well as recurring absenteeism due to

47. 2002 Annual Report, NYLPI available at www.nylpi.org/nylpi_2000-ar.pdf.

48. *Domestic Violence Survivors as Microentrepreneurs*, 12 AEO Exchange 6, Oct-Dec. 2003 *available at* www.microenterpriseworks.org/newsletter/Oct-Dec2003/Oct-Dec2003-FINALweb.pdf (last visited Feb. 6, 2004).

injury, and/or undermining the woman's self confidence and sense of competence. After exiting an abusive relationship and while healing from the abuse, microenterprise training and its support systems can foster economic independence for the woman and her children.

Another example of collaboration between microenterprise development and domestic violence is alt.Consulting's partnership with the Coalition Against Domestic Violence and the Rape Crisis Center in North Little Rock, Arkansas. Together, they work on safety planning issues for women who are currently being abused. In an abusive relationship, the opening of a business by the victim may be perceived as a threat to the abusive partner's domination and control. Microenterprise practitioners and legal counsel working with domestic violence survivors must understand the healing process for these women. Women often return to abusive relationships, and it is essential to have a solid support group in order to heal from domestic violence. Each state has a federally recognized domestic violence coalition. Lawyers and microenterprise staff could benefit from participating in training sessions offered by these state coalitions for persons who wish to better understand the problems of domestic violence.[49]

Thus, lawyers working with domestic violence survivors need to understand microenterprise development as one of various options that facilitate rebuilding and healing lives. Domestic violence survivors can benefit from guidance from their lawyers who can direct them to resources; microenterprise development is a resource in need of additional exploration. Furthermore, in reaching out to and collaborating with the domestic violence community, microenterprise development organizations may find new funding.[50]

Example

Elizabeth Stone House, a women's alternative mental health program in Boston, Massachusetts provides services to women who have experienced violence in their lives, including emergency shelter, transitional housing, and an economic self-sufficiency through its Community Education for Economic Development (CEED) program. CEED was created in response to program participants' needs, and promotes economic autonomy for domestic violence survivors

49. *Id.*
50. *Id.*

and their children in the Boston area through three methods: personal economic planning, the economic opportunity network, and the women's business opportunity program. CEED seminars "provide training to organizations working towards the creation of economic development initiatives within the communities that they serve." According to their mission statement, the "core of the Elizabeth Stone House philosophy is that women can succeed when empowered to maintain control over their own lives."[51]

4. *Physically Challenged Persons*

Thirty million American's have some kind of physical and/or mental disability.[52] Moreover, this population, America's largest minority, has a 70% unemployment rate and the potential to respond to self-employment better than any other group.[53] In spite of the 1990 passage of the American's with Disabilities Act, discrimination in the workplace against people with disabilities remains. The microenterprise industry recognized that self-employment is well suited to disabled persons, but it had not reached out to the disabled community in any specific way. However, this changed in 2000 when the microenterprise industry created the Abilities Fund.[54] The Abilities Fund expands to a national level the path-breaking work of the Entrepreneur with Disabilities Program in Iowa, which boasts a 90% stay-in-business sustainability for 160 start-ups and expansion businesses.[55]

The Abilities Fund is admittedly just one example of a partnership between the microenterprise industry and the disabled community, but entrepreneurship among disabled entrepreneurs can be encouraged in several ways. First, add "and people with disabilities" in the statement in program brochures about serving minorities. Unless the organization

51. This example was written by Kyle Waldner, George Washington University Law Student and Research Assistant to Prof. Jones, based on a telephone interview with Toni Jones of Elizabeth Stone House. For more information visit the Website at www.elizabethstonehouse.org or call (617) 522-3659.

52. The Abilities Fund Reaches An Overlooked Population, 4 AEO Exchange, Oct-Dec. 2001, *available at* www.microenterpriseworks.org/newsletter/Oct-Dec2001/Oct-Dec2001Web.pdf (last visited Feb. 6, 2004).

53. *Id.*

54. *Id.*

55. *Id.*

explicitly states that disabled people are included they will feel excluded. Second, microenterprise professionals may fear the cost of accommodating disabled persons and may not be comfortable because they do not feel they have the financial and other resources to make the accommodation. This can be addressed through information, familiarity, education, and experience. Third, microenterprise trainers must say out loud everything that is printed because not all disabilities are apparent.[56] As with other target groups, described in this chapter, lawyers can assist MED programs and clients with issues affecting disabled entrepreneurs.

5. Exoffenders

"Every year, society's institutions, communities and families must absorb an overwhelming number of released offenders. America's poorest communities, especially those of color, bear the brunt of the pervasive cycle of arrest, incarceration, and reentry. The impact of imprisonment and reentry has decimated many facets of community life: 1.5 million minor children have a parent in prison and poor communities can barely support the financial costs of prisoner re-entry. Sadly, statistics indicate that "nearly two-thirds of released prisoners are expected to be rearrested for a felony or serious misdemeanor within three years of release." The reasons for this "revolving prison door" are well understood. Many ex-offenders are released with little more than a bus ticket and a few dollars, and have no job prospects nor any real chance to better their lives. Some may have received high school equivalency diplomas or other job training education in prison, but find it difficult to employ those skills in today's workforce."[57]

In fact, research demonstrates that "[u]nemployed ex-convicts are three to five times more likely to commit another crime than those who are employed . . . .Yet it is especially difficult for ex-convicts to obtain employment, as their criminal records are viewed upon negatively by most hiring employers. . . . It follows that social policy programs which

---

56. *Id; See also* U.S. Department of Justice, Civil Rights Division, Disability Rights Section, Americans with Disabilities Act: ADA Guide for Small Business, *available at* www.usdoj.gov/crt/ada/smbusgd.pdf (last visited Feb. 6, 2004).

57. Jennifer Leavitt, *Walking a Tightrope: Balancing Competing Public Interests in the Employment of Criminal Offenders*, 34 Conn. L. Rev 1281 (2002).

would reduce the levels of unemployment among ex-convicts, and thus reduce recidivism, would be of benefit to society at large, since recidivism imposes major costs to society both objectively (the financial costs of both the crimes and the resulting incarcerations) and subjectively (high crime rates impose quality-of-life-tolls upon society). And because the objectives of increasing ex-convicts' employment *by others* faces such high hurdles, the alternative of fostering *self-employment* for ex-convicts is an important consideration."[58]

Rehabilitation through employment is one clear way to stem the tide of ex-offenders leaving and re-entering society through the jailhouse doors. Incarceration has not served society well as a method to reduce recidivism. However, facilitating employment opportunities for ex-felons may help to lower the recidivism rate by a significant percentage.

So, what is being done to help ex-offenders? On a broad level, scholars are evaluating the impact of entrepreneurial training programs on prison inmates;[59] foundations are supporting ex-prisoner reentry programs;[60] and faith-based organizations are assessing ways to re-absorb ex-offenders into communities.[61] A few microenterprise development programs have even implemented pilot self-employment programs in prisons.

But there are also some specific programs that have been successful in helping ex-offenders re-establish themselves in society. The Institute for Social and Economic Development (ISED)[62] and the Iowa Department of Corrections have collaborated on an innovative program funded by a grant from the Ms. Foundation for Women to train women in corrections facilities. Recognizing that many women ex-offenders will face insurmountable prejudices because of their criminal records, which in turn forces them to accept inadequate positions in low wage jobs with no benefits, microbusiness training is being introduced as a way to supplement low wage jobs and in some instances is the sole source

58. Matthew C. Sonfield, Robert N. Lussier and Robert J. Barbaro, The Entrepreneurial Aptitude of Prison Inmates and the Potential Benefit of Self-employment Training Program; *see also* Matthew C. Sonfield, From Inmate to Entrepreneur: A Preliminary Analysis, both on file with the author.

59. *Id.*

60. Michael Anft, *Seeking a Smooth Reentry: New Funds and Efforts Help Ex-Inmates Return to Society*, The Chronicle of Philanthropy, June 27, 2002. Michael Anft, *OffBeat Program's Success With Ex-Inmates Draws Notice*, The Chronicle of Philanthropy, June 27, 2002.

61. *See, e.g.*, Ruben Castaneda, Churches Ally Against Crime; Ivey Gives Faith Leaders a Role in Addressing Social Problems, Wash. Post, Nov. 20, 2003, at T05.

62. *See* www.ised.org (last visited Feb. 13, 2004).

of employment. As of December, 2003, the ISED ex-offender program has recruited 161 participants of whom 128 have completed training. Four businesses have been created.[63]

Similarly, New Visions, New Ventures (NVNV) a nonprofit 501(c)(3) organization committed to addressing the economic issues through training, job placement, and self-employment for income enhancement, works with the Fluvanna Correctional Center for Women in Virginia in an experimental demonstration project called Entrepreneurial Program for Transitioning Women (EPTW).[64] EPTW "centers on entrepreneurship as a viable economic development model for women transitioning from prison." NVNV started its Women's Economic Self-Sufficiency Initiative (WESI) in 1998 recognizing that 951,900 women nationwide were in the criminal justice system, 75% were in prison for nonviolent offenses, and that their reentry into society is inevitable. The average cost to taxpayers per inmate is $25,000 per year. Operating under WESI, the NVNV Entrepreneurial Program for Transitioning Women (EPTW) believes that entrepreneurship presents two "viable economic improvement options for transitioning women. The first is full-time self-employment or microbusiness activity. The second—and perhaps more realistic option for these women—is self-employment for income enhancement. By combining wages from a traditional job with earnings from self-employment activity, individuals can move towards economic self-sufficiency and greater economic independence."[65]

NVNV's president, a 20-year veteran entrepreneur, believes that NVNV's model, a work in progress, "has much potential for successfully reintegrating transitioning women into the community and its economy. Entrepreneurial activity enhances traditional sources of income, and women who develop a goal of self-employment become motivated and empowered to achieve economic self-sufficiency. . . . This combination of economic independence and positive self-esteem helps reduce their likelihood of re-incarceration."[66]

NVNV gained the recognition of the Virginia Assembly resulting in approval of a $45,000 planning grant in 1999 because of the program's potentially favorable economic impact enabling unproductive resources

---

63. Information on file with the author.

64. Patty Frost, *From Prisoner to Entrepreneur: An Enterprising Journey*, 3 MARKETWISE 14 (Community Affairs Office of the Federal Reserve Bank of Richmond 2001), *available at* www.rich.frb.org/cao/pdf/mwise2001-3.pdf (last visited Feb. 6, 2004).

65. *Id.*

66. *Id.*

to become productive in declining welfare rolls, contributions to the tax base, and a reduction in prison recidivism.

The program operates in two parts. In the first pre-release phase of the program, NVNV identifies participants and considers only those applicants who indicate an interest in self-employment and who are within six months to one year of release. Initial screening includes "entrepreneurial inventories, social histories, and personal interviews. Subsequent screenings include intensive psychological and social interviews."[67] The women selected participate in a Microentrepreneurial Training Program that combines financial literacy, microenterprise instruction and creative thinking exercises, as well as leadership development which "begins during the pre-release training and continues post-release with more formal instruction in leadership and opportunities for personal leadership experiences."[68] The training "encourages women to clarify values, examine their process of decision making, and learn to set short and long term goals, and map out a path for their future that includes economic self-sufficiency."[69] A goal of the program is to "help the women outline a vision of self-employment for their lives and then formalize the vision through the development of a business plan and exposure to information on microbusiness start up and operations."[70] Recognizing the need for immediate job placement, NVNV also explores job placement for each participant in an area related to her entrepreneurial interest. "Under the NVNV model, job placements offer income for daily sustenance while providing on-the-job training related to the participant's entrepreneurial interest."[71] The model also recognizes that by "stabilizing an individual's personal situation, you lessen the chances of employee turnover for an employer."[72] NVNV "works carefully to build trust relationships with potential employers and create opportunities that are supportive of the participant's self-employment goals."[73]

Upon release from prison, the women enter the Microbusiness Incubation Phase, the second part of the program. "In addition to job

67. *Id.*
68. *Id.*
69. *Id.*
70. *Id.*
71. *Id.*
72. *Id.*
73. *Id.*

placements, services include business counseling, technical assistance, computer training, mentoring, and leadership development."[74]

The program's outreach coordinator observes: "It is through systematic and collective partnerships between businesses, faith-based organizations, workforce development programs, counseling services, and the criminal justice system that this model is developed."[75]

6. Housing and Homelessness

The intersection between housing, anti-homelessness advocacy, and the creation of homeownership opportunities for low to moderate-income people is another growing aspect of the microenterprise industry.

Housing and homelessness are intertwined. Homelessness is caused by the shortage of affordable housing, poverty, low wage work insufficient to pay for basic living expenses, and the lack of supportive services to help people overcome personal challenges such as physical and/or mental health problems, and alcohol and substance abuse. Addressing the needs of homeless people today is a formidable task because the causes of homelessness are complex. Today, homeless people include women, families with children, the mentally ill, persons dependent on drugs and alcohol, and the unemployed. In fact, "Statistics show that: 10.5 million renters compete for 6.1 million low-income housing units; 4.4 million people lack an affordable place to live; at least 2.3 million Americans (nearly 1% of the U.S. population) are likely to experience a period of homelessness; 750,000 people are homeless on any given night; families with children make up 37% of homeless Americans and they are the largest group of homeless in rural areas; 14% of homeless people are veterans; 21% of homeless people are working; 14% are single women; 63% have suffered domestic violence by a male partner."[76]

Accordingly, anti-homelessness advocates and proponents of affordable housing are looking to the microenterprise industry to aid their efforts to assist clients with economic self-sufficiency initiatives including self-employment.

---

74. *Id.*

75. *Id.*

76. *See* Susan R. Jones, *Representing the Poor and Homeless: Innovations in Advocacy: Tackling Homelessness Through Economic Self-Sufficiency*, 19 St. Louis U. Public L. Rev. 385-386 (2000) (citing National Alliance to End Homelessness, Facts About Homelessness *at* www.naeh.org/back/factsys.html).

There are several examples of innovations in homelessness advocacy and microenterprise.[77] Lawyers who work in housing and homelessness can advance policy initiatives in housing and microenterprise.

Business lending in low-income communities is also beginning to influence housing finance for low-income people. Research sponsored, in part, by the Fannie Mae Foundation,[78] which examines the feasibility of replicating international finance models in the United States, refers to "microfinance for housing" as synonymous with low and moderate income lending. A growth area for the microenterprise industry, microfinance for housing combines two distinct paths of development in housing finance: low and moderate income (LMI) housing finance and microlending for housing. While LMI housing finance has its origins largely in the traditional financial sector, microlending for housing has "stemmed more directly from microenterprise lending."[79] Broadly defined, microfinance for housing "tries to accommodate households ranging from those with moderate income to the very poor by adapting sustainable approaches to their specific needs." While "microenterprise lending for income generation is a well-developed more and more commercialized field in emerging-market nations worldwide . . . [m]icrolending for housing . . . is a much more recent, less widespread aspect of microfinance—but a growing one."[80] There are three manifestations of this phenomenon: (1) Microenterprise loans used to upgrade and expand dwellings when the home is used for income generating activities; (2) as an explicit subset of LMI lending and microlending by banks and microlenders committed to housing and community development; and (3) as an offshoot of nonprofit housing organizations that add housing finance to their shelter projects.[81]

Microlending for low-income housing has been fueled by the Federal Housing Enterprises Safety and Soundness Act (FHESSA) and Com-

77. *See, e.g.*, Jones *supra* note 144 at 400 ("Focusing on growth occupations, for example, [t]he Salvation Army Woof Program (Work Opportunities for Outstanding Futures), 'provides low-income and no-income individuals with instruction in both dog training and business start up in a ten week training program.' ").

78. Fannie Mae Foundation creates affordable homeownership and housing opportunities through innovative partnerships and initiatives that build healthy, vibrant communities across the United States." For more information visit the Fannie Mae Foundation Website *at* www.fanniemaefoundation.org. (last visited Feb. 6, 2004); *see also* JAMES H. CARR AND ZHONG YI TONG, REPLICATING MICROFINANCE IN THE UNITED STATES 259 (2002).

79. Carr, *supra* note 136, at 259.

80. *Id.*

81. *Id.*

munity Reinvestment Act of 1977 and amendments to the act. FHESSA places more pressure on Fannie Mae and Freddie Mac, government sponsored entities (GSEs) that lend to homebuyers, to serve low income and minority families and neighborhoods.[82]

Another way that the issues of affordable housing intersect with microenterprise development is as part of a self-employment strategy for residents of public and subsidized housing programs.

Affordable housing legal advocates representing the homeless as well as those representing public housing authorities can advance opportunities for microenterprise development.

7. Arts, Crafts, Food Specialty Items, Entertainment, and Tourism

Lawyers can also provide legal assistance to microenterprise programs and microbusinesses enabling entrepreneurship though arts, crafts, specialty food items, entertainment, and tourism. Lawyers have represented microenterprises such as local music bands, storytellers, lamp designers, and groups of entrepreneurs promoting ethnic arts.

The microbusiness industry promotes sectoral markets, encouraging groups of entrepreneurs in crafts, specialty food items, the textile and fashion industries, as well as in other creative areas to work together to purchase supplies and sell their products. In some communities cultural tourism provides business opportunities.

A good illustration of such programs is Rosie's Place. Located in Boston's South End, it created the Women's Craft Cooperative, a program in which women whose lives have been waylaid by poverty or homelessness fashion boutique quality jewelry and accessories from buttons.[83] A 67-year-old senior cooperative member and a resident of one of Rosie's Group apartments has worked at the cooperative for five years. She remembers being "sick and homeless in Boston eight years ago, when she was down to her last $10.00."[84]

82. *Id.* at 275–76.

83. Irene Sege, *Creating Button Jewelry, Women Fashion New Lives,* BOSTON GLOBE, Dec. 21, 2002, at D1.

84. *Id.*

"Most women come to the cooperative without a crafts background. The program costs the nonprofit Rosie's Place $150,000 a year to run. In strict business terms—direct sales and orders from vendors—the cooperative has yet to break even although . . . [it] expects to bring in more than the $80,000 it collected last year. Add the button profits that businesses such as J. Jill and Frugal Fannie's now donate to Rosie's Place, and the cooperative should cover its expenses for the first time in its history."[85]

Rosie's Place is just one example of the important intersection of microbusiness, housing and social services. Furthermore, it is an example of social entrepreneurship—"'a provocative blend of social, philanthropic and business values' which is an integration of social work, community economic development and business development in the creation of social purpose businesses."[86]

Other examples include The Aspen Institute's Access to Markets Learning Assessment and the Appalachian Center for Economic Networks. The Aspen Institute's initiative was funded in conjunction with the Mott Foundation's 1998 grant to seven microenterprise practitioner organizations. Access to Market (ATM) services have the goal of "connecting entrepreneurs to additional or previously inaccessible customers, thereby increasing sales of and possibly income from the business."[87] The Appalachian Center for Economic Networks (ACEnet) in rural Ohio created a Food Venture project to assist microenterprises in the natural and specialty food sectors. In 1999 the specialty and natural food market had more than $48 billion in sales with an estimated 5% real growth rate.[88]

Lawyers working with nonprofit organizations that run businesses must ensure that they maintain their federal tax exemption and comply with local regulations while engaging in profit making business ventures.

---

85. *Id.*

86. Jones, *supra* note 98 at 407 (citing The Roberts Foundation, New Social Entrepreneurs: The Success, Challenge and Lessons of Non-Profit Enterprise Creation, A Progress on the Planning and Start-Up Nonprofit Businesses from the Roberts Foundation, Homeless Economic Development Fund 2-3 (1996)).

87. Mary McVay and Madi Hirschland, *The Aspen Institute, Access to Markets Case Study Series/No. 1, Making the Connection: Appalachian Center for Economic Networks* (ACEnet) (Sept. 2000).

88. *Id.*

8. Faith-Based Programs

The current administration's faith-based initiative has raised many legal and policy questions.[89] AEO Executive Director Bill Edwards observes that "faith-based microenterprise members are doing some of the best work in maintaining the focus on poverty alleviation as the most important impact of U.S. microenterprise efforts."[90]

A number of religious institutions may wish to start microenterprise development organizations. A preliminary question requiring legal analysis is whether to start a separate corporation and seek 501(c)(3) tax exemption from the Internal Revenue Service. Many lawyers and CED support organizations, such as The National Congress For Community Economic Development (NCCED), have developed training materials to assist groups with this question and urge the creation of a separate legal entity.[91] Lawyers can also advise organizations on regulatory and statutory interpretations.

Faith-based microenterprise happens in several ways. First, various faiths have economic justice initiatives seeking to address the root causes of poverty and as a result, support CED and microenterprise initiatives. For example, the American Bishops' Pastoral Letter of 1986, Economic Justice for All, observes that the "deprivation of the powerless and the poor wounds the whole community."[92] Similarly, the Episcopal Network for Economic Justice supports CED activity to address society's "systematic injustices" that "perpetuate poverty and lack of access to resources."[93] In Judiasm, Lirdof Tzedec is the obligation to do justice and according to Maimonides, a Jewish sage, the greatest level of tzedekah "is to strengthen the hand of the poor by

89. Irshad Abdal-Haqq, Faith-Based Initiatives and Muslim Community Development: Part 1: Federal Funding of Faith-Based Organizations: Issues and Considerations: Part 2 The Muslim Faith-Based Community Development Corporation as a Vehicle for Progress (2001); *see also Faith Based Microenterprise, Part 1: Government Funding,* 8 AEO Exchange Oct.-Dec. 2002; *Part II: How is Faith-Based Microenterprise Different?,* 9 AEO Exchange Jan-Mar. 2003.

90. *See also Faith Based Microenterprise, Part 1: Government Funding,* 8 AEO Exchange Oct.-Dec. 2002; *Part II: How is Faith-Based Microenterprise Different?* 9 AEO Exchange, Jan-Mar. 2003, at 3.

91. *See* www.NCCED.org (last visited Feb. 13, 2004).

92. *See* www.episcopal.church.org/peace-justice/enej.

93. *Faith Based Microenterprise Part II: How is Faith-Based Microenterprise Different?* 9 AEO Exchange Jan.-Mar. 2003 at 3; *see also* Florence Wagman Roisman, *The Lawyer as Abolitionist: Ending Homelessness and Poverty in Our Time,* 19 St. Louis U. Pub. L. Rev. 237 (2000).

means of gift or loan or by going into partnership with him so that he can become self-sufficient."[94]

Second, secular organizations partner with religious groups. For example, The Philadelphia Development Partnership's microenterprise program reaches out to churches, mosques, and synagogues and has created special financial products in compliance with Islamic laws, which prohibit changing interest.[95]

The Association for Enterprise Opportunity (AEO) has identified a number of trends in faith-based microenterprise organizations (FBMOs), represented among every major religious faith in the nation—Catholics, Jews, Protestants, and Islamics—are approximately 10% of microenterprise development organizations and this number is growing. The fact that some organizations have faith-based origins may not be apparent in the name. They generally receive financial support from a religious body and most are organized as separate 501(c)(3) tax-exempt organizations. The clientele of FBMOs are low and moderate income and the base clientele is often not related to the religious roots. FBMOs are more likely to have a poverty alleviation focus to their work than non-FBMOs.

9. Youth Microenterprise

Youth-centered microenterprise development, a component of the broader field of youth entrepreneurship, can assist America's young people in becoming self-employed. It can also teach economic literacy and consumer awareness while promoting human capital and leadership development.[96]

Organizations such as the National Foundation for Teaching Entrepreneurship (NFTE) help students demystify the business world and train students to be business literate. As NFTE's executive director observes, "Poverty is transcended by those who possess knowledge and who know how to create value. . . . The problem with education . . . is that we teach children the tools of economic participation, the how, but fail to clarify or make relevant the why."[97]

94. *Id.*

95. *Id.*

96. American Bar Association's Steering Committee on the Unmet Legal Needs of Children, America's Children Still At Risk 456-457 (2001).

97. *Id.*

"Lawyers can play a valuable role in promoting microenterprise for young people. Lawyers can counsel individual youth entrepreneurs in issues such as establishing worker cooperatives and drafting cooperative agreements. Lawyers working with youth in areas such as special education, criminal justice, and other fields can be important resources for identifying useful and innovative models for youth entrepreneurship and training for self-employment."[98]

Example

The Prudential Foundation created the Prudential Young Entrepreneur Program (PYEP) in Newark, New Jersey and Philadelphia, Pennsylvania in 1999. Since that time, over 200 individuals have graduated from the nine-week entrepreneurial fundamental skills course. Participants range in age from 18 to 30. The program not only teaches basic business development to young entrepreneurs, but also often ultimately creates jobs for its graduates.

Managed by the AEO, the PYEP capitalizes on local resources: the Enterprise Development Center, Inc., of the New Jersey Institute of Technology (NJIT-EDC, Newark), and The Enterprise Center, affiliated with the University of Pennsylvania's Wharton School of Business in West Philadelphia provide the training course and technical assistance. In Philadelphia, The Enterprise Center also serves as microlender, while in Newark, the Greater Newark Business Development Consortium performs the same role.

Successful graduate businesses include two award winning companies: a golf and gear company run by Newark graduate A.J. Nolten, and a marketing promotions company for hairstylists and braids run by Philadelphia graduate Michael Green.

Students laud the education they receive at the PYEP. "The program is geared toward people who probably wouldn't have this opportunity to make a dream become a reality," said Danean Jacobs-Eme, owner of Sunshine Daycare Center and a 1999 graduate of the PYEP.

98. *Id.*

The program was originally conceived as a three-year pilot project but its great success has encouraged the Prudential Foundation to extend its grant until 2005.[99]

10. Rural Communities

Rural America is diverse. Statistics show that rural areas are home to 56 million people, contain 80% of the Nation's land, and comprise more than 2,300 counties in various communities, climates and geographies. Despite this diversity, rural areas have many common characteristics. They tend to be some of the poorest regions and are located distances from urban centers, thus hindering economic activity. They are sparsely populated and have experienced a decline in natural resource-based industries on which they have traditionally relied. Globalization, resulting in plant closings, is making it increasingly difficult for low-skilled and undereducated people in rural areas to find jobs. Rural areas are also increasingly populated by legal immigrants.[100] Moreover, rural microenterpreneurs experience limited access to consumer markets, low wealth local markets, capital shortages, and a lack of technology. Rural entrepreneurs need to build niche and sectoral markets, and to develop access to markets.[101]

In an effort to better understand the special challenges and opportunities of rural entrepreneurship, W.K. Kellogg Foundation in collaboration with the AEO created a two-year learning cluster on rural policy. The purpose of this initiative is to support the capacity of rural microenterprise programs to advance local policy objectives.[102]

---

99. Kyle Waldner prepared this example. Prudential Young Entrepreneur Program, available at www.microenterpriseworks.org/projects/PYEP/PYEPmain.htm.

100. Association for Enterprise Opportunity (AEO), Microenterprise Development in the Rural United States *at* www.microenterpriseworks.org/about/factsheets/Rural-Fact-Sheet.PDF (last visited Feb. 16, 2004).

101. *Id.*

102. AEO Learning Cluster: Rural Policy *at* www.microenterpriseworks.org/projects/ruraldevelopment/RuralPolicy.htm (last visited Feb. 16, 2004). The Learning Cluster Participants are: The Appalachian Center for Economic Networks (ACEnet), Ohio; The Center for Rural Affairs, Nebraska; Central Vermont Community Action Council, Inc. (CVCAC), Vermont; The Institute for Social and Economic Development (ISED), Iowa; The Legal Assistance to Microenterprise Project (LAMP), Texas; West Company and Jefferson Economic Development Institute (JEDI), California.

Researchers have found that knowledge of small business in rural areas is limited.[103] According to the Heartland Center, "Thriving rural communities believe their destiny is in their own hands. Making their communities good places is a pro-active assignment, and they willingly accept it."[104]

Lawyers can make a contribution to creating self-employment jobs through microenterprise development in rural communities. The Center for Rural Entrepreneurship encourages Entrepreneurial Support Organizations (ESOs), which can include networks, intermediary organizations, and industry clusters. ESOs have three significant attributes. First, they place primary focus on entrepreneurs rather than enterprises. Second, they create a support system that nurtures the entrepreneur through stages of business development while providing resources, tools, and guidance. Legal support is a critical part of this process. Third, they contribute to the creation of an entrepreneurial environment that is supported by the public and private sector.[105]

Among other sources, funding support for rural microenterprises comes from the U.S. Department of Labor, Employment and Training Administration and the U.S. Department of Agriculture.[106]

11. Native American Communities

"While efforts to promote entrepreneurship among low income communities nationwide have grown dramatically over the past twenty years, only recently has Indian country begun to benefit from these programs and services."[107] The Native American Entrepreneurship Project of the First Nations Development Institute estimates that 170,083 of the 197,300 Native American–owned businesses reported in the 1997

---

103. Kirk C. Heriot, Eileen A. Hogan and Joan M. Kendall, Growth of Small Business: Issues Related to Success and Failure in Rural America, *available at* www.sbaer.uca.edu/Research/1999/SBIDA/99sbi230.htm (last visited Feb. 6, 2004).

104. 20 Clues to Rural Community Survival: An Annotated List *at* www.heartlandcenter.info/clues.htm (last visited Feb. 16, 2004).

105. Organizations such as the Rural Enterprise Assistance Project and the Rural Assistance Center can also provide helpful resources.

106. George Wallace, *Using Microenterprise Programs in the Rural United States*, Rural America, Jan. 2000 at 38, *available at* www.ers.usda.gov/publications/ruralamerica/RA151/RA151F.PDF (last visited Feb. 16, 2004).

107. CFED, Entrepreneurship Development in Native American Communities, Corporation for Enterprise Development (on file with the author).

census are microbusinesses. Although these statistics should be a source of pride in Indian Country, observers say that these numbers are not accurate, and greater efforts must be made to support Native American businesses.[108]

Tribal governments play a critical role in community economic development initiatives on Indian reservations. Groups such as the Oregon Native American Business & Entrepreneurial Network (ONABEN) were created to increase the success of private businesses owned by Native Americans and to provide individualized training to Indians on business development.[109]

As with other target populations, Native American communities could benefit from transactional legal assistance to help promote microenterprise development and as part of a larger community economic development strategy.

E. Dissolution of Microenterprise Programs: A Case Study[110]

Sometimes MED programs are unable to sustain themselves for a variety of reasons and must cease business operations. A microenterprise program contemplating dissolution should communicate with its funding sources (stakeholders) and competitors as soon as possible about a decision to dissolve. It should review the terms of grant and loan obligations so that it can comply with all obligations, and carefully review its cash flow situation to ensure that it has sufficient funds to complete the dissolution process.

The Coalition for Women's Economic Development (CWED) recently embarked on just such a process. Founded in 1988, CWED was

108. Jeff Hinkle, *The Business of Small Business: While Lawmakers consider the future of one Overlooked Agengy, Native Groups make Headway*, AMERICAN INDIAN REPORT, July, 2002, at 12.

109. David D. Haddock and Robert J. Miller, Economic Development in Indian Country: Can A Sovereign Nation Protect Creditors From Itself? Tribal Institutions to Reservation Investment (Oct. 2003) (unpublished paper presented at the Ninth Annual Lewis & Clark Business Law Forum, Perspectives on Community Economic Development, Lewis & Clark Law School, on file with the author); *see also* www.onaben.org.

110. Andrea Ball and Peter Manzo drafted this section, based on interviews with Mari Riddle, former Executive Director of CWED, and Lori Freeling, a Public Counsel volunteer attorney who represented CWED in its dissolution.

one of the first organizations in Southern California to offer microloans and training. In its relatively short eight-year lifespan, CWED was very successful both in serving its clients and raising awareness of the need for access to capital for microbusinesses and small business entrepreneurs in Los Angeles and beyond. CWED's efforts helped spur the creation of numerous microenterprise and small business lenders in Southern California. Indeed, the development of alternative resources for its clients was an important factor on which CWED relied in determining that it had largely fulfilled its original mission and in deciding to dissolve. The issues CWED faced in winding down provide important lessons for those considering dissolution.

CWED was an early participant in the U.S. Small Business Administration's (SBA) Microloan Demonstration Project (MDP). The interest rate on CWED's loan from the SBA was significantly higher than the interest rates offered to later MDP participants. Therefore, CWED ended up charging higher interest rates on its microloans to microbusinesses than other microlenders. By 1996, CWED found that a number of other organizations in its service area were able to offer similar loans at lower interest rates.

An additional consideration for CWED was that the MDP required matching funds and did not provide for payment of indirect costs. CWED had to aggressively raise funds to cover overhead costs of administering the SBA MDP programs, and to obtain the 15 to 20% matching funds, in addition to raising funds for CWED's other privately funded lending activities. By the mid-1990s, the competition in Southern California for private funding, especially for operating costs became intense, and CWED decided the time had come to cease activity.

One of the first steps in CWED's dissolution was to provide for the organization's largest debt, its MDP loan from the SBA. Upon being notified of CWED's intention to discontinue participation in the MDP and cease operations, the SBA immediately exercised its lien on the CWED bank accounts containing SBA funds—a Microloan Revolving Fund and a Loan Loss Reserve Fund—and applied these amounts to the balance of the outstanding loan.

The SBA's stance was that CWED must immediately repay the entire loan balance, approximately $50,000, despite the fact that much of this balance was tied up in a portfolio of well-performing loans CWED made under the MDP loan agreement. CWED had the option to sell its loan portfolio and, provided all funds due to CWED from the purchaser were paid directly to the SBA, the SBA would agree to release its lien on those loans. CWED, however, would still be responsible for any balance remaining after the sale of the portfolio.

CWED attempted to find a nonprofit organization willing to buy its portfolio, which at the time was valued at approximately $90,000. A nonprofit economic development organization offered to assume the obligations of CWED under the promissory note and loan agreement with SBA and to administer the loan portfolio. A second organization offered $26,000 to purchase the portfolio at a discount. CWED chose the assumption option. After significant wrangling with SBA officials in both Los Angeles and Washington, D.C., CWED obtained SBA approval to transfer all obligations under the note and loan agreement as well as the administration of the loan portfolio to the economic development organization.

The Los Angeles office of the SBA administered the assignment of CWED's participation in the MDP to the assuming organization. The SBA provided and signed a form Assumption Agreement pursuant to which CWED assigned its obligations under the note, loan agreement, and security agreement to the nonprofit economic development organization which expressly assumed those obligations. Although this transfer cleared CWED's obligation to repay the outstanding loan balance, the SBA would not allow assumption of the entire approved MDP loan amount, which CWED had not fully drawn down. Rather, only the outstanding balance could be assumed by the non-profit economic development organization. Accordingly, the assignee could not make new loans with SBA funds, it could only administer the existing loans. Presumably, if the assignee demonstrates adequate administration of the portfolio, it will increase its chances of being selected by the SBA to participate in the next phase of the Microloan Demonstration Program.[111]

F. Merger of Microenterprise Programs

Although some programs find it necessary to dissolve, others may find that merging with another microenterprise program or another non-

111. The Microloan Program is now a permanent SBA program, *see* The Facts About . . . The Microloan Program for Entrepreneurs at www.sba.gov/opc/pubs/fs68.pdf (last visited Sept. 7, 2004).

profit group is a viable alternative to a precarious existence. As practitioners identify community needs, resources, and funding options, programs may determine that they need to refocus target populations, for instance, from displaced workers to welfare recipients. Thus, they might undertake an analysis of the nonprofit organizations in the region to determine whether one of these groups might absorb such a program.

For example, a church-based community center in Washington, D.C., which provides space to a wide range of nonprofit organizations providing teen mentoring, a free health clinic, food for the homeless, and low cost housing, hopes to attract a microenterprise program to increase self-sufficiency options for the low-income and immigrant community it serves. The prospect of a nonprofit merger raises complicated legal questions requiring careful review of the financial and legal status of the organizations involved.

CHAPTER 5

Funding Microenterprise Programs

Funding is perhaps the most challenging task in instituting microenterprise programs. Unfortunately, there is no exact formula to obtain funding. However, hard work, networking, careful investigation, and creative alliances between nonprofit groups may aide the eternal quest for funding. New funding opportunities may also emerge as the microenterprise movement continues to grow and its successes are documented.

A. Socially Responsible Investments

Fueled by concerns about the fundamental responsibilities of corporations in South Africa, the movement toward socially responsible investments began in the 1960s. Questions about the fundamental responsibilities of corporations in society drove this movement. Ethical investment allows individuals and institutions to practice their belief that investing can be based on social and moral values as well as the financial bottom line. Today, the ethical investment movement estimates that more than a half a trillion dollars is invested according to some form of ethical judgment.[1]

Attorneys and legal organizations can contribute to enterprise development initiatives by considering long-term investments in programs that support microentrepreneurs. Program related investments (PRIs)

1. *See* Council on Economic Priorities et al., The Better World Investment Guide (1991); Joel Makower, Beyond the Bottom Line: Putting Social Responsibility to Work for Your Business and the World (1994).

can allow these programs to stretch their asset base, thus expanding their impact. A legal organization can make direct market-rate investments in loan guarantee funds, direct loans to microenterprise programs at negotiated rates, or equity investments in programs that issue stocks. The appropriate method depends on the degree of risk and desired rate of return. Attorneys can assist microenterprise programs to explore avenues for leveraging community economic development with finance capital.

Organizations such as the Calvert Social Investment Fund (CSIF) make investments in enterprises that contribute to society through their products or services. One CSIF initiative called the High Social Impact Investment Program, which has gained over $2.5 million in investments since 1990, has financed microenterprise initiatives. Through its Social Investment Foundation, The Calvert Group has launched a feasibility study on funds devoted to high impact investing.[2]

Legal organizations and attorneys can use this kind of investment strategy to contribute to microenterprise initiatives while earning a return on investment. A resource list for socially responsible investing is located in the Appendix.

B. Revolving Loan Funds

A revolving loan fund (RLF) is a financial vehicle for lending money for community-based projects considered "risky" by conventional sources. By matching socially concerned investors with capital, RLFs borrow capital and re-lend it on affordable terms to benefit communities. The return on investments in RLFs may be less than market rate, but unlike some other investments, they improve communities. For example, the average investment in one community based RLF is $5,000, which would earn 5% interest or $250 per year compared with a 3.5% rate of interest which would earn $175 per year. Some investors could

2. The Calvert Social Investment Fund allocates a small portion of assets for investments that create jobs, affordable housing, and credit opportunities at local levels. For more information visit their Website at www.calvertsif.com (last visited Apr. 19, 2004). The Calvert Group also contains Cascadia Revolving Fund, a nonprofit loan fund that helps small businesses expand throughout the Pacific Northwest. The Appendix of this handbook includes more information on all of these resources.

easily conclude that the difference of $75 per year is well worth the contribution to community.[3]

C. Community Development Financial Institutions

Community Development Financial Institutions (CDFIs) are private sector, locally controlled financial institutions that provide credit, training, and technical assistance to niche markets that conventional financial institutions do not serve in economically distressed communities. They include a broad range of regulated and unregulated institutions including community development banks, community development credit unions, community development loan funds, and community development venture capital funds. As unconventional lenders, their primary mission is to ensure community development by supporting areas such as job creation, microenterprise development, affordable housing and encouraging savings in low-income areas.[4]

D. Venture Capital

Venture capital issues for nonprofit organizations are different than for-profit organizations. In the for-profit corporate world, a venture capital firm will have a great influence on the business operations by holding an equity interest (owning a part of the company). Furthermore, the return on the investment is generally more; in other words, it yields a higher interest rate. Most venture capital firms only want to invest in fully operational companies when they can demonstrate significant unrealized market potential or the ability to develop new markets. Nonprofit organizations, on the other hand, resemble new entrepreneurs whose start-up (or growth capital) will come from personal savings, credit cards, home mortgages, family, or friends. Nonprofits are largely

3. For more information about RLFs and similar organizations, contact the National Community Capital Association, 924 Cherry St., Philadelphia, PA 19107-2411 or (215) 923-4754.

4. *See* Rochelle E. Lento, *Community Development and Banking Strategy for Revitalizing Our Urban Communities*, 27 U. Mich. J.L. Reform, 773, 776 (1994).

dependent on foundation grants to cover new business exploration and development. Seed capital funds have been established recently to provide start-up capital for high-risk business ventures.

E. Program Related Investments

PRIs are very low interest loans made by a foundation (generally from its endowment) to a nonprofit organization. They are an important source of start-up financing for earned income ventures. PRIs vary in form, represent hybrid-financing tools, and are an important source of start-up financing for earned income ventures.

Most microenterprise programs would agree that financing their operations is a difficult task which can only be improved with help from many sources. The legal community has a vital role to play in financing by helping microenterprise programs understand issues from board liability to unrelated business income tax, as well as the legal issues involved in establishing a for-profit subsidiary.[5]

F. Private Sector Resources

Private sector financial institutions that are Federal Home Loan Bank (FHLBank) members may access a discounted source of funds that can be lent for microenterprise activities. The FHLBanks lend Community Investment Program (CIP) advances (loans) to their thrift and commercial bank members at interest rates that are 15 to 50 basis points below the rate usually charged for FHLBank advances. The financial institution members use the CIP funds to provide loans to their customers for commercial and economic development activities that benefit low and moderate-income households or that are located in low and moderate-income neighborhoods. Microenterprises may use CIP funds to finance lines of credit, to acquire or rehabilitate office buildings, and in combination with SBA or other public loan guarantees.

---

5. *See*, e.g., Christie I. Baxter, Program-Related Investments: A Technical Manual for Foundations (1997); Peter C. Brown, The Complete Guide to Money Making Ventures for Nonprofit Corporations (1986); Alceste T. Pappas, Reengineering Your Nonprofit Corporation: A Guide to Strategic Transformation (1995).

CHAPTER 6

Legal and Business Issues for Microbusinesses

A. Getting Started: Legal Entity Choices

There are many types of legal entity choices for new small businesses. The majority of microbusinesses are organized as sole proprietorships because they are the simplest form of doing business. The only documents needed to create a sole proprietorship may be a local tax registration, a federal employer identification number,[1] a trade name, a fictitious name, "doing business as" (DBA) or "trading as" (T/A) designation, and a license or permit if required.[2]

Some types of microbusinesses, such as construction contractors or trucking companies, may produce a greater likelihood of lawsuits. As a result, these and other retail businesses may want to limit their liability. Sometimes the business can get insurance to limit its exposure to lawsuits, but this may not be enough. Because of the uncertainty associated with liability exposure, some microbusinesses may want to choose a

1. Sole proprietors can use their personal Social Security numbers or obtain a separate Federal Tax Identification Number (EIN).

2. A trade name, fictitious name, doing business as or trading as designation is usually required when the business has a name other that the name of its owner. For example, if Donna Smith operates a retail trash hauling service called "Trash Toppers," she might need to file a document with the state or local government indicating that Donna Smith is doing business as or trading as "Trash Toppers."

business entity that provides limited liability such as a corporation, a limited liability company, or a limited liability partnership.

There are two different types of corporations for tax purposes: S corporations and C corporations. Each has very specific requirements but simply stated, an S Corporation is taxed as a conduit in a manner that is similar to a partnership. In a C corporation, there are two layers of taxation: at the corporate level and when dividends are paid to the shareholders (owners of the corporation).

Another legal entity option for new small businesses is the Limited Liability Company (LLC) which offers partnership tax treatment with the benefit of limited liability. An LLC is simpler to establish and maintain than a corporation.[3]

B. Business Plan

A business plan is a road map which explains how to legally structure, manage, market, and finance the business. Most microentrepreneurs learn about these areas from the program they are enrolled in and many programs require the development of a comprehensive business plan as part of microenterprise training.[4]

C. Contracts

Microentrepreneurs will often be parties to loan agreements. Thus, business and banking lawyers engaged in helping microentrepreneurs with business agreements must strive to create legally enforceable contracts that are clear to persons with little formal education. In some instances letters of agreement may be sufficient. Moreover, there are common

3. *See* Phillip L. Jeslma, *How Do LLC's Stack Up: A Point by Point Comparison with S and C Corporations*, Bus. Law Today, Mar./Apr. 1995, at 32, 33; Larry E. Ribstein, *The Emergence of the Limited Liability Company*, 51 Bus. Law. 1, 2–3 (1995); *Guide to Limited Liability Companies* (CCH ed. 1999). The Journal of Limited Liability Companies can also be a source of useful information.

4. *See* David H. Bangs, Jr., The Business Planning Guide: Creating a Plan for Success in Your Own Business (1995). This book is available from Upstart Publishing Company, a division of Dearborn Publishing, 155 N. Wacker Dr., Chicago, IL 60606-1719; (800) 235-8866.

agreements that microentrepreneurs may need such as service contracts, lease agreements, and employment agreements.[5]

D. Licenses and/or Permits

State and localities often require a license or permit to engage in a particular occupation, profession, or enterprise, or to operate a business in a particular zone of the city. For instance, operating a home based business, running a dry cleaning establishment, operating as a barber or a beauty shop, etc., may require licenses or permits.

E. Insurance

Insurance is an important way to protect a microbusiness and its owner. Fire, casualty, theft and general liability insurance are some basic forms of insurance. State and federal law generally require workers' compensation and unemployment insurance. Other types of business insurance are business interruption and key person insurance. Home-based businesses should be sure that business equipment is insured separately from the home or apartment because renters' or homeowners' insurance does not generally cover business equipment in the home unless there is a special insurance rider. Finally, the individual owner may need health or life insurance.

F. How Microbusinesses Can Protect Their Work

Although the following protection issues may not concern all microbusinesses, intellectual property protection is becoming increasingly important.

5. Useful contract drafting resources for lawyers and their clients include: STEVEN C. ALBERTY, ADVISING SMALL BUSINESSES (1995); SCOTT J. BURNHAM, DRAFTING CONTRACTS (1995); PETER SIVIGLIA, WRITING CONTRACTS (1996); FRED. S. STEINGOLD, THE LEGAL GUIDE FOR STARTING AND RUNNING A SMALL BUSINESS (1995); LEGAL GUIDE FOR SMALL BUSINESS, (The American Bar Association 2000.)

1. Copyright

Copyright is the protection given to authors of original works, and protects the author from others using the work without permission.[6] Copyright law applies to literary, musical, dramatic and other artistic works such as dance and motion pictures.

To be copyrightable the work must be original, reflect creative authorship, must be produced by the author's own intellectual effort, and must not be copied from another. Copyright does not protect ideas, systems, methods, concepts, principles, or information that is standard, common, or contains no original authorship, such as calendars or height and weight charts. Copyright also does not protect works in which the creative authorship is too slight: names, titles, slogans, short phrases, variation of different types, lettering or color, blank forms, and similar works intended to record information rather than convey it, or works of the United States Government.

Contrary to popular belief, a person does not need to "register a copyright" to get copyright protection. Copyright protection attaches as soon as the work is created "or fixed in a tangible medium," e.g., as soon as the words are put on paper. Still, registration of copyright protects important rights of the microbusiness owner.

Authors of original works should place copyright notice on the work (this is not legally required but it can be helpful). This can be done by writing: (1) ©, copyright or copr.; (2) the first year of publication of the work; and (3) the name of the owner of the copyright in the work or an abbreviation by which the name can be recognized, e.g., © 2004 David Diaz.

Copyright registration is a legal formality intended to make a public record of the basic facts of a particular copyright. It is not a condition to copyright protection, but registration makes a public record of the copyright claim. Thus, it is ordinarily necessary before an infringement suit may be filed in court. If made within five years of publication, registration provides prima facie evidence in court of the validity of the

6. Provisions for copyright are written into the Constitution of the United States in the Patent and Copyright Clause. Art. I, cl. 8 of the Constitution, which states: "The Congress shall have the power . . . to promote the Progress of Science and useful arts, by securing for limited Times to Authors and Inventors the exclusive right to their respective Writings and Discoveries." Over time the terms "author" and "writings" have been broadly interpreted to include areas such as choreography and sculpture.

copyright and the facts stated in the certificate; registration made within three months after publication of work or prior to infringement allows statutory damages and attorneys' fees to be available to the copyright owner in court actions.[7]

At $30, basic copyright registration is relatively inexpensive. Copyright lasts for the life of the author plus 70 years.[8]

2. Trademarks/Service Marks

Trademarks and service marks create product recognition. A trademark is any word, name, or symbol adopted for use by a merchant or manufacturer to identify goods and distinguish them. Examples of trademarks include Coca-Cola® and Microsoft®. A service mark is used in the sale or advertising of services to distinguish them from the services of another.[9]

Trademarks should be distinguished from corporate names or trade names. The formal name of a business is its trade name. The name that a business uses to market its product or services is called a trademark or a service mark. For example, Cadillac® and Chevrolet® are registered trademarks of General Motors Corporation.

Trademarks do not have to be registered and when used in commerce are protected by common law. However, important benefits to federally registering a trademark include exclusive nationwide ownership of the mark, official notice to all later users of the mark that it is already taken, the right to put ® after the mark, the right to make the mark "incontestable" by keeping it in continuous use for five years after

---

7. If the work has not been registered, damages are limited to only actual damages. Actual damages are measured by how much the business was hurt or how much money in profits the infringer made. Statutory damages range between $250 and $10,000 and may reach $50,000 if the infringement is willful. There is a $100 minimum if the defendant is not aware and had no reason to believe he or she was infringing.

8. For more information, call the Library of Congress Copyright Public Information Office at (202) 707-3000 for Circular 1—Copyright Basics and other publication or visit the Copyright Office Website at www.copyright.gov.

9. Federal Trademark Registration is governed by 15 U.S.C. §§ 1051, 1052–72, 1091–96, 1111–21, 1123–27, 37 C.F.R. Part 2, and The Trademark Manual of Examining Procedure. For general information 1123–27, 37 C.F.R. Part 2, and The Trademark Manual of Examining Procedure. For general information that is useful to microbusinesses, see EVERYONE'S GUIDE TO COPYRIGHTS, TRADEMARKS, AND PATENTS (1990) and KATE MCGRATH ET AL., TRADEMARK: HOW TO NAME A BUSINESS & PRODUCT, 2d ed. (1996). PATENT, COPYRIGHT & TRADEMARK: AN INTELLECTUAL PROPERTY DESK REFERENCE, 6th ed. (2003).

the date of registration, and the presumption of ownership in the case of litigation involving the mark. If a mark is not federally registered, the symbols TM (for trademark) or SM (for service mark) may be used.

Although trademark rights may last indefinitely, between the fifth and sixth year of use of the federally registered mark, the owner of the mark must file an important document called "Section 8 Affidavit" that advises the Patent and Trademark Office (PTO) that the mark is still in use and that the federal registration of the trademarks is still in force.

A trademark may also be registered at the state level. Microbusinesses that are unable to afford the cost of federal registration ($335 for one classification of goods) may want to obtain a state trademark registration to claim ownership in the mark. A benefit of state registration is that it puts other local businesses on notice of the mark's use. A comprehensive trademark search should reveal the existence of the mark so that other businesses become aware of the state registration.[10]

3. Patents

A patent protects an invention and is a property right given by the U.S. Government to the inventor. The term of the patent is 17 years from the date the patent is granted, provided maintenance fees have been paid. Unlike trademarks and copyrights, it is very difficult for an individual to pursue a patent application without legal assistance. An important piece of advice for an inventor is to keep your ideas secret.

Microentrepreneurs should be aware of invention promotion companies which, for a fee, claim to evaluate the patentability of an invention.[11] Instead, consult the American Intellectual Property Law Association, which publishes the book *How to Protect and Benefit From Your Ideas.*[12]

---

10. For more information about trade marks, contact the U.S. Department of Commerce, Patent and Trademark Office, Box Trademark, Washington, D.C. 20231. Call (703) 415-HELP (4357) for general information on Patent or Trademark or visit the PTO Website at www.uspto.gov.

11. The Inventor's Digest offers information about patenting inventions. Contact Inventor's Digest at 4859 Gallery Road, Suite 209, Colorado Springs, CO 80915; Fax (719) 573-4679; E-mail: Inventors@aol.com; Website: www.inventorsdigest.com.

12. Available from the American Intellectual Property Law Association, 2001 Jefferson Davis Highway, Suite 203, Arlington, VA 22202, (703) 345-0780; www.aipla.org/Content/ContentGroups/Publications1/Publications_available_for_viewing1/howto.pdf (last visited Feb. 6, 2004). For more information on patents consult the PTO Website at www.uspto.gov.

4. *Royalties*

A royalty is a payment (or a form of income) based on the use of property. For example, if the microbusiness is a franchise, the franchiser gets a royalty in the amount of a percentage of the income the franchise earns. This income is usually a percentage of gross sales not profits.

5. *Licenses*

A license is permission to use property, such as a license to use a trade name or to reproduce a written work. Another good example of a license would be a kiosk stand, which have become popular in malls and other spaces, that may sell anything from T-shirts to jewelry and coffee. The microentrepreneur engaged in this type of business may enter into a license agreement to use the space in the mall.

6. *Trade Secrets*

Trade secrets are information about the business such as a special recipe for a sauce or a muffin, its customer list, or the special process it uses. In order to be a trade secret the information must be truly secret (e.g., the recipe cannot be in a published recipe book), and it must be protected (e.g., by having employees sign written confidentiality agreements that the information is secret).

G. Taxes

Microbusinesses must be sure to comply with applicable tax laws. Many new businesses fail because they do not file tax returns, keep proper records, or pay IRS income tax withholding for employees. Microbusiness owners should keep a daily record including business expenses and business receipts. Furthermore, there are tax benefits from running a legitimate business, such as the home office deduction, automobile costs and other business expenses (e.g., computer and telephone costs).[13] For a comprehensive list of tax publications, see *A Guide to Tax Services*, which can be obtained from the IRS.[14]

H. Working with Others (Independent Contractors and Employees)

Microbusiness owners will often work with two types of people who, hopefully, will help the enterprise prosper: employees and independent contractors.

First, it is important to understand whether it is proper to classify a worker as an independent contractor or employee. An employer must withhold state and federal tax for an employee and pay the employer's share of payroll taxes. An independent contractor pays her own state and federal taxes. Because no employer wants to pay taxes, many employers would prefer to classify a worker as an independent contractor as opposed to an employee. Most workers cannot be classified as independent contractors. As a general rule, the Internal Revenue Service (IRS) looks to the degree of control that the employer has (or can have) over the worker. A business can get a determination from the IRS about whether a worker is an independent contractor or an employee by filing form SS8-Determination of Employee Work Status for Purposes of Federal Employment Withholding Taxes and Income Withholding. IRS penalties for misclassification can be costly.[15] In addition, whether a person is an independent contractor or an employee will have an impact on other legal areas such as workers compensation and unemployment insurance.

---

13. *See* Dan Meyer, Account for Your Own Success: Everything You Need to Manage Your Own Business and Personal Finances 36-38 (1993) (containing explanations for categories of business expenses); *see also* Jane Bryant Quinn, *Sometimes Shelters Can be Scams,* Wash. Post, June 30, 1996, at H2; Jane Bryant Quinn, *Taking Legal Home Business Deductions,* Wash. Post, July 7, 1996, at H2.

14. The IRS can be contacted at 1 (800) 424-FORM or www.ustreas.gov/prod/cover.html.

15. The Small Business Job Protection Act of 1996, 26 U.S.C. § 1 (1996), adds important safe harbor provisions under section 530 of the Revenue Act of 1978. These provisions, which became effective on January 1, 1997, provide employer's relief from liability if the employer can show a reasonable basis for treating the employee as an independent contractor. *See* Internal Revenue Service, U.S. Dep't. of the Treas., Publication No. 1976, Independent Contractor or Employee?, available at www.irs.gov/pub/irs-pdf/p1976.pdf (last visited Apr. 19, 2004).

I. Alternative Dispute Resolution

Suing is expensive for everyone involved. In addition, sometimes there are legitimate reasons for default and easy solutions to appease both sides. Therefore, it is important for microenterprise lenders and borrowers in default to consider negotiating and settling disputes without litigation or going to court. Thus, all parties should consider alternative dispute resolution, which involves either mediation or arbitration.[16] Mediation is a process by which a neutral third person helps the parties to a dispute reach agreement. Arbitration is the process by which an individual or a small panel (usually three persons) decides the outcome of a dispute. Arbitration may be binding (final) or it may be nonbinding (a court may still hear the case). An arbitration panel may consist of lawyers and/or experts in the field who know about "industry standard" or what is customary in the field.

16. For more information contact the American Arbitration Association (AAA). 140 West 51st St., New York, NY 10020-1203; Tel: (212) 484-4000; Fax: (212) 765-4874; Website: www.adr.org. The AAA also has a Commercial Mediation Center or contact the Society of Professionals in Dispute Resolution (SPIDR), International Office, 815 15th Street, NW, Suite 530, Washington, D.C. 20005; Tel: (202) 783-7277; Fax: (202) 783-7281; Website: www.igc.apc.org/spidr; or the American Bar Association Section of Dispute Resolution, 740 15th Street, NW, Washington, DC 20005; Tel: (202) 662-1690.

CHAPTER 7

The Future of Microenterprise: Trends, Direction, and Legal Issues

The September 11, 2001 terrorist attacks have forever changed the face of America and the fundamental nature of international relations. Economist Muhammed Yunus, known as banker to the poor and advocate of microenterprise development, argues that access to credit is a human right. Indeed, legal scholars and policy makers concerned about the less fortunate among us are examining a plethora of issues regarding banking and the poor.[1]

By all accounts from practitioners, policy makers, and legislators, microenterprise development will play a significant role in future domestic economic development initiatives. In recent years alone, the microenterprise development industry has witnessed the First Presidential Awards for Excellence in Microenterprise Development sponsored through the Community Development Financial Institution Fund (CDFI) and the International Microcredit Summit, which brought together over 2,000 people from around the world to celebrate microenterprise development and to work toward the objective of reaching one million microbusinesses. Studies to date provide important evidence of the strength of microenterprise as a development strategy. Microenterprise advocates are still assessing and evaluating their vision for microenterprise in the future. Legal issues abound including fund raising, joint ventures and other capacity building arrangements with community-based organizations, banks, credit unions and other businesses. These relationships are essential for sustaining the industry. The microenterprise community also has a strong legislative agenda to in-

1. Michael S. Barr, *Banking and the Poor*, 21 Yale J. on Reg. 121 (2004).

crease state and local government awareness of the role of self-employment in job creation and community economic development.

Lawyers practicing in areas as diverse as domestic violence, disabilities, business, banking, civil rights, and welfare will play a critical role in assisting the microenterprise industry as it grapples with achieving its goals of assisting America's most needy entrepreneurs.

Supporters of microenterprise development believe that diversity and strong community ties will be central to the growth of the industry. A range of program models will contribute to the human, economic, and community development impacts that public and private investors will expect in providing continuous support for the industry.

Appendix

Microenterprise Resources

A. Organizations That Support Microenterprise

ACCION International
56 Roland Street, Suite 300
Boston, MA 02129
Tel: (617) 625-7080
Fax: (617) 625-7020
Email: info@accion.org
Website: www.accion.org

Since 1961, ACCION International has enabled the self-employed poor to achieve economic self-reliance. By providing the basic tools of credit and training, it offers a helping hand to these "microentrepreneurs" struggling to survive on meager incomes earned from cottage industries. Dedicated to helping people help themselves, ACCION is making dramatic strides in fighting hunger and poverty in Latin America and the United States.

Aspen Institute
Self Employment Learning Project (SELP)
One Dupont Circle, N.W.
Suite 700

Washington, DC 20036-1133
Tel: (202) 736-5800
Fax: (202) 467-0790
Email: See Website
Website: www.aspeninst.org

The Aspen Institute designed SELP, a multi-year research and evaluation effort, to produce new information and encourage dialogue on the field of self-employment and microenterprise development as a poverty alleviation and employment creation strategy. SELP develops and shares evaluation tools with the practitioner community as well as disseminates project findings to practitioners, funders, and the policy community.

Association for Enterprise Opportunity (AEO)
1601 N. Kent Street
Suite 1101
Arlington, VA 22209
Tel: (703) 841-7760
Fax: (703) 841-7748
Email: aeo@assoceo.org
Website: www.microenterpriseworks.org

The AEO is a national trade association of organizations committed to microenterprise development. It provides its members with a forum, information, and a voice to promote enterprise opportunity for people and communities with limited access to economic resources. AEO also represents the U.S. microenterprise agenda in the growing international community.

The Calvert Foundation
4550 Montgomery Avenue, N. 100
Bethesda, MD 20814
Tel: (800) 368-2748
Fax: (301) 951-4860
Email: customerservice@calvert.com
Website: www.calvertgroup.com

The Calvert Foundation invests in the skills and tenacity of hard-working, low-income people around the world who want to create new businesses and jobs, buy their own homes, or revitalize their neighborhoods. It places investments that make the critical difference to people working their way out of poverty by providing the necessary capital.

Cascadia Revolving Loan Fund
1901 NW Market Street
Seattle, WA 98107-3912
Tel: (206) 447-9226
Fax: (206) 682-4804
Email: info@cascadiafund.org
Website: www.cascadiafund.org

Cascadia Revolving Fund (CRF) is a nonprofit community development financial institution. Incorporated in 1985, Cascadia provides financial and technical assistance (e.g., accounting, legal, or marketing assistance) to both for-profit entrepreneurs and nonprofit organizations who are engaged in a community building activity but who are not able to find financing from traditional sources. CRF won one of seven Inaugural Presidential Awards for Excellence in Microenterprise Development.

Corporation for Enterprise Development
777 North Capitol Street, N.E.
Suite 800
Washington, DC 20002-4239
Tel: (202) 408-9788
Fax: (202) 408-9793
Email: cfed@cfed.org
Website: www.cfed.org

The Corporation for Enterprise Development promotes broad, sustainable economic wellbeing. It offers policy design, analysis and advocacy, demonstration and project management, consulting, technical assistance, training, research, information and publication services to public, private, nonprofit and community organizations in the United States and abroad.

Development Alternatives, Inc.
7250 Woodmont Avenue
Suite 200
Bethesda, MD 20814
Tel: (301) 718-8699

Fax: (301) 718-8699
Email: info@dai.com
Website: www.dai.com

Development Alternatives, Inc., recognizes the importance of small business and helped pioneer "best practice" thinking in micro and small enterprise development. It offers expertise in enterprise and institutional development, marketing and market development, policy reform, privatization, agribusiness, trade and investment promotion, credit and finance, and information systems. From 1989 through 1995, DAI worked with USAID on a project called Growth and Equity Through Microenterprise Investments and Institutions (GEMINI). GEMINI publications are available through Pact Publications (Website: www.pactpub.com/geminipub.html). DAI is now working with USAID on the Microenterprise Innovation Project which is related to the GEMINI project (Website: www.mip.org).

Foundation for International Community Assistance (FINCA)
FINCA USA, Inc.
1101 14th Street, N.W.
11th Floor
Washington, DC 20005
Tel: (202) 682-1510
Fax: (202) 682-1535
Email: info@villagebanking.org
Website: www.villagebanking.org

FINCA supports the economic and human development of families trapped in severe poverty. It achieves this by creating "village banks" which are peer groups of 20 to 50 members, predominantly women, which offer loans for self-employment activities and a support system that encourages self-worth.

Manpower Demonstration Research Corporation
19th Floor
16 East 34th Street
New York, NY 10016-4326
Tel: (212) 532-3200
Fax: (212) 684-0832

Email: information@mdrc.org.
Website: www.mdrc.org

The Manpower Demonstration Research Corporation is a nonprofit, nonpartisan research organization that develops and evaluates innovative approaches to moving people from welfare to work. It helps build a stronger workforce through training, revitalizing low-income communities, and improving secondary education for at-risk youth.

Charles Stuart Mott Foundation
Mott Foundation Building
503 S. Saginaw Street
Suite 1200
Flint, MI 48502-1851
Tel: (810) 238-5651
Fax: (810) 766-1753
Email: info@mott.org
Website: www.mott.org

The C.S. Mott Foundation is a grant making organization that supports efforts to promote a just, equitable, and sustainable society.

Ms. Foundation for Women
120 Wall Street
33rd Floor
New York, NY 10005
Tel: (202) 742-2300
Fax: (202) 742-1653
Email: info@ms.foundation.org
Website: www.ms.foundation.org

The Ms. Foundation for Women is a national, multi-issue, public women's fund that supports the efforts of women and girls to govern their own lives and influence the world around them. It funds and assists women's self-help organizing efforts and directs resources to breaking down barriers based on race, class, age, disability, sexual orientation, and culture.

The National Community Capital Association
Public Ledger Building

620 Chestnut Street
Suite 572
Philadelphia, PA 19106
Tel: (215) 923-4754
Fax: (215) 923-4755
Email: ncca@communitycapital.org
Website: www.communitycapital.org

The National Community Capital Association, formerly the National Association of Community Development Funds, is a financial intermediary that assists private, nonprofit community development financial institutions. These institutions provide credit, capital, and technical assistance to assist the revitalization of low-income communities.

The National Congress for Community Economic Development (NCCED)
1030 15th Street, N.W.
Suite 325
Washington, DC 20005
Tel: (202) 289-9020
Fax: (202) 289-7051
Email: ncced@ncced.org
Website: www.ncced.org

The National Congress for Community Economic Development brings together nearly 700 community-based and community controlled development organizations which focus on economic development in low and moderate income communities of rural and urban America. It helps people achieve lasting economic viability by promoting community-based development industry.

Public Counsel Law Center
Office Address:
601 South Ardmore Avenue
Los Angeles, CA 90005
Mailing Address:
P.O. Box 76900
Los Angeles, CA 90076
Tel: (213) 385-2977
Fax: (213) 385-9089

Email: e-mail@publiccounsel.org
Website: www.publiccounsel.org

Public Counsel Law Center, as the nations largest pro bono law firm, provides a diverse range of services to low-income individuals, families, communities and organizations. In the area of community development, Public Counsel provides assistance to nonprofit organizations, works with affordable housing developers and tenants to create or preserve quality low-income housing, and provides pro bono business law assistance to low-income entrepreneurs.

Responsibility for Ending Starvation Using Legislation (RESULTS)
440 First Street, N.W.
Suite 450
Washington, DC 20001
Tel: (202) 783-7100
Fax: (202) 783-2818
Email: results@results.org
Website: www.results.org

RESULTS is a non-profit, grassroots citizen's lobby that identifies sustainable solutions to the problems of hunger and poverty. It works to generate the resources necessary to make those solutions succeed throughout the world, as it did at the Microcredit Summit. The Summit launched a campaign to extend credit for self-employment to the world's poorest families and the RESULTS Educational Fund is committed to supporting the initiatives begun at the Summit.

National Economic Development and Law Center (NEDLC)
2201 Broadway
Suite 815
Oakland, CA 94612-3024
Tel: (510) 251-2600
Fax: (510) 251-0600
Email: pubinfo@nedlc.org
Website: www.nedlc.org

NEDLC, established in 1969, is a non-profit public interest law and planning organization that specializes in community economic capacities of low-income communities and their residents.

B. Federal Agencies That Provide Microenterprise Assistance

U.S. Department of Health and Human Services
Office of Refugee Resettlement
Administration for Children and Families
Office Address:
901 D Street, S.W.
6th and 8th Floors
Washington, DC

Mailing Address:
370 L'Enfant Promenade, S.W.
6th Floor/East
Washington, DC 20447
Tel: (202) 401-9246
Fax: (202) 401-5487
Email: See Website
Website: www.acf.dhhs.gov/programs/orr/mission/dcr.htm

The Office of Refugee Resettlement's Refugee Assistance Program provides assistance to help refugees achieve economic self-sufficiency and social adjustment within the shortest possible time after arrival in the United States. Money and medical assistance, as well as social services that provide English language and employment training, are important parts of this program.

U.S. Department of Housing and Urban Development (HUD)
Community Development Block Grant Program
451 7th Street, S.W.
Washington, DC 20410
Tel: (202) 708-1122
Fax: (202) 401-2044
Email: See Website
Website: www.hud.gov/communitydevelopment/programs/index.cfm

HUD's Community Development Block Grant Program (CDBG) awards grants annually to states and entitled communities. CDBG allows grant recipients to address local community development concerns based on issues of primary importance to them. Through active citizen participation, communities develop their own funding priorities and then plan and execute activities that will address those priorities.

U.S. Department of the Treasury
Community Development Financial Institution Fund
601 13th Street, N.W.
Suite 200, South
Washington, DC 20005
Tel: (202) 622-8662
Fax: (202) 622-7754
Email: cdfihelf@cdfi.treas.gov
Website: www.cdfifund.gov and www.cdfi.gov/programs/BEA

The Community Development Financial Institution (CDFI) Fund was created "to expand the availability of credit, investment capital and financial services in distressed urban and rural communities." A bipartisan initiative authorized by Riegle Community Development and Regulatory Improvement Act of 1994, the Fund's investments work toward building private markets, creating healthy local tax revenues, and empowering residents by infusing small amounts of capital into institutions that serve distressed communities and leveraging private-sector investments from banks, foundations, and other funding sources. Since its creation, CDFI has made more than $300 million in awards to community development organizations and financial institutions.

CDFI also sponsors the Bank Enterprise Award (BEA) Program, which recognized the key role played by traditional financial institutions in community development lending. The program is intended to encourage banks and thrifts to invest in and support community development financial institutions (CDFIs) and to increase the lending and services provided in distressed communities by traditional financial institutions.

U.S. Department of the Treasury
Office of the Comptroller of the Currency
Independence Square
250 E Street, S.W.
Washington, DC 20219-0001
Tel: (202) 874-5000

Fax: (202) 874-4950
Email: See Website
Website: www.occ.treas.gov

The Office of the Comptroller of the Currency is an independent bureau of the Treasury Department that oversees the nation's federally chartered banks. It furnishes Community Reinvestment Act evaluations of banks allowing residents to determine which banks are reinvesting in their communities. It also provides useful information on banking in general.

U.S. Small Business Administration
National Office
409 3rd Street, S.W.
Washington, DC 20416
Tel: (800) U-ASK-SBA
Fax: (202) 205-7064
Email: See Websites
Websites: Small Business Administration, www.sba.gov; U.S. Small Business Advisor, www.business.gov

For a list of U.S. Small Business Development Centers on the Internet: www.sba.gov/gopher/Local-Information/Small-Business-Development-Centers

The SBA Microloan Program is currently the largest and most visible federal program dedicated solely to microenterprise development. The SBA makes loans to community-based microlenders to capitalize revolving loan funds and awards grants to support technical assistance associated with the microlending.

C. Nonprofit Resource Organizations

Association of Fundraising Professionals (formerly National Society of Fund Raising Executives)
1101 King Street
Suite 700
Alexandria, VA 22314

Tel: (703) 684-0410
Fax: (703) 684-0540
Email: See Website
Website: www.afpnet.org

The National Society of Fund Raising Executives (NSFRE) is the professional association for individuals responsible for generating philanthropic support for a wide variety of not-for-profit, charitable organizations. Founded in 1960, NSFRE promotes consistent and high standards of professional practice to ensure donor trust and guard against abuses which can occur in the fundraising process.

Board Source (formerly National Center for Nonprofit Boards)
1828 L Street, N.W.
Suite 900
Washington, DC 20036-5114
Tel: (202) 452-6262 or (800) 883-6262
Fax: (202) 452-6299
E-mail: See Website
Website: www.ncnb.org

Board Source is the only nonprofit organization dedicated to building stronger nonprofit boards and stronger nonprofit organizations. It exists to help nonprofit leaders board members and paid executive staff engineer healthy, powerful organizations. Board Source provides the resources, leadership tools, and answers to help people become better nonprofit leaders.

The Foundation Center
79 Fifth Avenue/16th Street
New York, NY 10003-3076
Tel: (212) 620-4230; (800) 424-9836
Fax: (212) 807-3677
Email: See Website
Website: fdncenter.org

The Foundation Center is an independent nonprofit information clearinghouse established in 1956. The Center's mission is to foster public understanding of the foundation field by collecting, organizing, analyzing, and disseminating information on foundations, corporate giving, and related subjects. The audiences that call on the Center's resources include grant seekers, grant makers, researchers, policymakers, the media, and the general public.

National Center for Nonprofit Law
1735 20th Street, N.W.
Washington, DC 20009
Tel: (202) 462-1000
Fax: (202) 462-1001
Email: See Website
Website: www.nonprofitlawcenter.org

The National Center for Nonprofit Law informs nonprofit staff, lawyers, trustees, and volunteers about legal, financial and organizational issues facing nonprofit institutions.

D. Legal Nonprofit Bibliography

Books published by John Wiley & Sons, N.Y. in their Nonprofit Law, Finance and Management Series, (800) 753-0655:

Jody Blazek, Tax Planning and Compliance for Tax Exempt Organizations: Forms, Checklists, Procedures (3rd ed. 1999).

Tracy Daniel Conners, The Volunteer Management Handbook (1999).

Malvern J. Gross, Jr., et al., Financial Accounting Guide for Not-for-Profit Organizations (6th ed. 2000).

Bruce R. Hopkins, Starting and Managing a Nonprofit Organization: A Legal Guide (3rd ed. 2000).

Bruce R. Hopkins, Charity, Advocacy and the Law (1991).

Bruce R. Hopkins, The Law of Fund-Raising (2nd ed. 1996).

Bruce R. Hopkins, The Legal Answer Book for Nonprofit Organizations (1996).

Bruce R. Hopkins, The Second Legal Answer Book for Nonprofit Organizations (1998).

Bruce R. Hopkins, Nonprofit Law Dictionary (1994).

The Nonprofit Counsel (Bruce R. Hopkins ed.). This is a monthly journal.

The Nonprofit Handbook: Management (Tracy Daniel Connors ed., 2001 & Supp. 2002).

Alceste T. Pappas, Reengineering Your Nonprofit Organization: A Guide to Strategic Transformation (1995).

Seth Perlman & Betsy Hills Bush, Fund-Raising Regulation: A State-by State Handbook of Registration Forms, Requirements and Procedures (1996 & Supp. 2000).

Publications by the National Economic Development and Law Center (2201 Broadway, Suite 815, Oakland, CA 94612; (510) 251-2600; Fax: (510) 251-0600; HandsNet: HN0186):

Taking the Entrepreneurial Approach: A Resource Guide for Nonprofits. (Contains information on the venture development process; feasibility studies and business plans; financing; legal issues such as operating a business by a nonprofit; community based organizations and unrelated business income; alternative loan fund support for CED ventures).

Community Economic Development Strategies: Creating Successful Businesses. (Three-volume set.) (1983) Order no. 1900-8.

Useful books by other publishers:

Barbara L. Kirschten, Nonprofit Corporation Forms Handbook (2002), West Group, Eagan, MN (800) 328-9352, (800) 328-4880, (651) 687-7000.

Anthony Mancuso, How to Form a Nonprofit Corporation (5th ed. 2002). Nolo Press (800) 992-6656, (831) 466-9922. Includes a list of state corporation offices.

Mihailo Temali, The Community Economic Development Handbook: Strategies and Tools to Revitalize Your Neighborhood (2002).

E. Resource Bibliography for Microenterprise Programs

The following self-help business books are useful in assisting microbusinesses. Because some microenterprise programs work with low-income and low-educated persons, it is important to ensure that legal concepts are explained in non-legalistic ways.

Anatomy of a Start-Up: Why Some Businesses Succeed and Others Fail (Elizabeth K. Longsworth, ed., 1991); ISBN: 0-9626146-6-1

Janet Attard, The Home Office and Small Business Answer Book (2nd ed. 2000); ISBN: 0-8050-64508

David H. Bangs, Jr., The Start Up Guide: A One-Year Plan for Entrepreneurs (3rd ed. 1998); ISBN: 1574101153

E. Thorpe Barrett, Write Your Own Business Contracts: What Your Attorney Won't Tell You (James E. Mahan, ed., 3rd ed. 2000); ISBN: 1555714870

Business Resource Guide for the 90's available from The Business Resource Center, 940 Adams St., Suite E, Benicia, CA 04510, (707) 747-1018

Everyone's Guide to Copyrights, Trademarks, and Patents (1990); ISBN: 0-894-71-752-9

William A. Hancock, The Small Business Legal Advisor (2nd ed. 1991); ISBN: 0070260028

Philip Holland, How to Start a Business Without Quitting Your Job (1992); ISBN: 0-89815-449-9

Claudia Jessup & Genie Chipps, The Woman's Guide to Starting a Business (revised ed. 1979); ISBN: 0-8050-0871-3

Kate McGrath, et al., Trademark: How to Name a Business and Product (2nd ed. 1996); ASIN: 0873373111

Anthony Mancuso, Form Your Own Limited Liability Company (Beth Lawrence, ed., 2002); ISBN: 0873377974

Dan Meyer, Account for Your Own Success: Everything You Need to Manage Your Own Business and Personal Finances (1993); ISBN 0-932150-04-7

Fred Steingold, The Employer's Legal Handbook: A Complete Guide to Your Legal Rights & Responsibilities (5th ed. 2003); ISBN: 087337844x

Fred Steingold, The Legal Guide for Starting & Running a Small Business (7th ed. 2003); ISBN: 0-87337-9101

Paul Adams, Legal Do's (& Don'ts) for the Small Business (1996); ISBN: 047113161X

Roy S. Alonzo, Upstart Guide to Owning & Managing a Bar or Tavern (1994); ISBN: 0936894679

Arthur Andersen LLP, Small Store Survival: Success Strategies for Retailers (1996); ISBN: 0471164682

Arlene Appelbaum, Start Your Business Now! (1997); ISBN: 1885750048

Lynie Arden, Work-at-Home Sourcebook (8th ed. 2002); ISBN: 091178117x

Michael L. Baird, Engineering Your Start-Up: A Guide for the HiTech Entrepreneur (1999); ISBN: 0912045485

Veltisezar B. Bautista, How to Build a Successful One-Person Business (2nd revised ed. 1995); ISBN: 0931613124

Steven J. Bennett, Ecopreneuring: The Complete Guide to Small Business Opportunities (1991); ISBN: 0471530743

Rick Benzel, Making Money in a Health Service Business on Your Home-Based PC (2nd ed. 1997); ISBN: 0079131395

Gustav Berle, SBA Hotline Answer Book: Answers To The 200 Most Commonly Asked Questions Of The Small Business Administration (1992); ISBN: 0471542970

Leonard Bisk, Entrepreneur Magazine: Guide to Professional Services (1997); ISBN: 0471155179

Irving L. Blackman, Passing Your Business on to Your Family: Creating a Lifetime Succession Plan to Meet your Changing Tax, Estate and Business Needs (1995); ISBN: 1557388989

James W. Botkin & Jana B. Matthews, Winning Combinations: The Coming Wave of Entrepreneurial Partnerships Between Large & Small Companies (1992); ISBN: 047153658X

Steven C. Brandt, Entrepreneuring: The 10 Commandments for Building a Growth Company (3rd ed. 1997); ISBN: 1888925027

Anita Brattina, Diary of a Small Business Owner: A Personal Account of How I Built a Profitable Business (1995); ISBN: 0814402917

Hattie Bryant, Beating the Odds: Small Business 2000 (1996); ISBN: 0761503447

Irving Burstiner, Mail Order Selling: How to Market Almost Anything by Mail (3rd ed. 1995); ISBN: 0471097594

William D. Bygrave, Portable MBA in Entrepreneurship (3rd ed. 2003); ISBN: 0471271543

William A. Cohen, Building a Mail Order Business: A Complete Manual For Success (1991); ISBN: 0471520829

William A. Cohen, Entrepreneur & Small Business Marketing Problem Solver (1991); ISBN: 0471531332

Fred W. Daily, Tax Savvy for Small Business (7th ed. 2003); ISBN: 0-87337-9721

Will Davis, Start Your Own Business for $1,000 or Less (1994); ISBN: 0936894709

George M. Dawson, Borrowing to Build Your Business: Getting Your Banker to Say Yes (1997); ISBN: 1574100734

Dearborn Enterprise Directory of Small Business Success (1993); ISBN: 0793107806

Royce Diener, How to Finance a Growing Business (5th ed. 2000); ISBN: 1-563437007

Stephen & Janelle Diller, How to Succeed With Your Own Construction Business (1999); ISBN 0934041598

Jeffrey Dobkin, How to Market a Product for Under $500 (2001); ISBN: 0-9642879-2-7

Peter E. Drucker, Innovation & Entrepreneurship: Practice & Principles (1999); ISBN: 0887306187

Paul & Sarah Edwards, Working from Home (5th ed. 1999); ISBN: 0874779766

Christopher Egerton Thomas, How to Open & Run a Successful Restaurant (2nd ed. 1995); ISBN: 0471042366

Ann Graham Ehringer, Make Up Your Mind: Entrepreneurs Talk About Decision-Making (1995); ISBN 1-56343-101-7

Entrepreneur Magazine, Small Business Advisor (1995); ISBN: 0471109894

Gregory K. Ericksen, What's Luck Got to Do with It?: 12 Entrepreneurs Reveal the Secrets Behind Their Success (1997); ISBN: 0471179981

David R. Eyler, Home Business Bible: Everything You Need to Know to Start & Run Your Successful Home-Based Business (1994); ISBN: 0471595780

Stephen Fishman, Hiring Independent Contractors: The Employer's Legal Guide (3rd ed. 2000); ISBN: 0-87337-5769

Jack Fox, Starting & Building Your Own Accounting Business (3rd ed. 2000); ISBN: 0471351601

Roger Fritz, Small Business Troubleshooter: 152 Solutions for Problems Faced by Every Growing Company (2nd ed. 2000); ISBN: 1588320014

George Fuller, The First Time Supervisor's Survival Guide (1994); ISBN: 0133114325

Michael Gerber, E-Myth Revisited: Why Most Small Businesses Don't Work and What to Do About Yours (1995); ISBN: 0887307280

Davis Gersick & Lansberg Hampton, Generation to Generation: Life Cycles of the Family Business (1997); ISBN: 087584555X

Seth Godin, Point & Click Business Builder: Windows Version (1996); ISBN: 1574100548

Arnold Goldstein, J.K. Lasser's Legal & Corporation Forms for the Smaller Business (2nd ed. 1994); ISBN: 0671883275

Grant Seekers Guide: Foundations that Support Social and Economic Justice (Morris & Adler, eds., 6th ed. 2002); ISBN: 1559213043

David E. Gumpert, How to Really Start Your Own Business (4th ed. 2003); ISBN: 0970118163

Cliff Hakim, We Are All Self-Employed: New Social Contract for Working in Changed World (1995); ISBN: 18810524796

Robert Half, Making it Big in Data Processing (1987); ISBN: 0517565803

Wilson Harrell, For Entrepreneurs Only (1995); ISBN: 1564141934

Phaedra Hise, Growing Your Business Online: Small Business Strategies for Working the World Wide Web (1996); ISBN: 0805047387

Priscilla Y. Huff, 101 Best Home-Based Businesses for Women: Everything You Need to Know About Getting Started on the Road to Success (3rd ed. 2002); ISBN: 0761528172

Jasinowski & Hamrin, Making it in America: Proven Paths to Success from Fifty Top Companies (1995); ISBN: 0671507567

Michael D. Jenkins, Starting & Operating a Business in California: Step by Step Guide (9th ed. 1995); ISBN: 1555713726

Bernard Kamoroff, Smalltime Operator: How to Start Your Own Small Business, Keep Your Books, Pay Your Taxes, & Stay Out of Trouble (7th ed. 2000); ISBN: 0917510186

Erwin J. Keup, Mail Order Legal Guide (2nd ed. 1993); ISBN: 1555711901

Jan B. King, Business Plans to Game Plans: A Practical System for Turning Strategies into Action (2nd ed. 2000); ISBN: 1-56343-7015

David Langendoen & Dan Costa, Home Office Computing Handbook (1994); ISBN: 0830645772

David Lord & National Business Employment Weekly, Guide to Self-Employment: A Round Up of Career Alternatives Ranging from Consulting & Professional Temping to Starting or Buying a Business (1996); ISBN: 0471109185

Donald E. Lundberg, Hotel and Restaurant Business (6th ed. 1994); ISBN: 0442012462

Mike McKeever, How to Write a Business Plan (6th ed. 2002); ISBN: 0-87337-8636

Bess Ritter May, Starting & Operating Business After You Retire: What You Need To Know To Succeed (1993); ISBN: 0895295679

Gerri P. Norington, The Road to Self-Employment (1997); ISBN: 1-890499-00-5

Ira N. Nottonson, Secrets to Buying and Selling a Business (3rd ed. 1999); ISBN: 1555714897

Patrick D. O'Hara, SBA Loans: Step By Step Guide (4th ed. 2002); ISBN: 0471207527

Patrick O'Hara, SBA Microloan & Specialty Handbook (1996); ISBN: 0471139149

Michael Phillips & Salli Rasberry, Marketing Without Advertising (4th ed. 2003); ISBN: 0-87337-9306

Linda Pinson & Jerry Jinnett, Starting Your Home-Based Business (2nd ed. 1996); ISBN: 0793116937

Linda Pinson, & Jerry Jinnett, Steps to Small Business Start Up: Everything You Need to Know to Turn Your Idea Into a Successful Business (5th ed. 2003); ISBN: 0793179270

Richard M. Turitz & Michael Cross, Prentice Hall Small Business Survival Guide: Blueprint for Success (1993); ISBN: 0130453293

Dave Radin, Building a Successful Software Business (1994); ISBN: 1565920643

Peter Rainsford & David H. Bangs, Jr., Restaurant Planning Guide: Starting And Managing A Successful Restaurant (2nd ed. 1996); ISBN: 1574100262

Dan Ramsey, Owning and Managing a Mail-Order Business: The Upstart Guide (1995); ISBN: 0936894970

Vickie Reierson, Start Your Business: Beginner's Guide (3rd ed. 1999); ISBN: 1555714854

Kelly Reno, 77 No Talent No Experience & (Almost) No Cost Businesses You Can Start Today (1995); ISBN: 0761502467
Russell Robb, Buying Your Own Business: An Adam's Business Advisors, Identifying Opportunities, Analyzing True Value, Negotiating the Best Terms (1995); ISBN: 155850544X
Lisa Angowski Rogak, & David H. Bangs, One Hundred Best Retirement Businesses (1994); ISBN: 0936894547
Marilyn Ross & Ross, Big Ideas for Small Service Businesses: How to Successfully Advertise, Publicize, & Maximize Your Business or Professional Practice (1994); ISBN: 0918880165
Jim Schnell, Entrepreneur Magazine Small Business Answer Book: Solutions to the 101 Most Common Small Business Problems (1996); ISBN: 0471148423
Lloyd E. Shefsky, Entrepreneurs Are Made Not Born: Secrets From 200 Successful Entrepreneurs (1994); ISBN: 0070570256
A. David Silver, Venture Capital Sourcebook: The Definitive Guide To Finding StartUp Funds & Growth Capital (1994); ISBN: 1557385580
Julian L. Simon, How to Start & Operate a Mail-Order Business (5th ed. 1993); ISBN: 0070575657
Daniel Sitarz, Complete Book of Small Business Legal Forms (3rd ed. 2000); ISBN: 0935755845
Small Business Forum, Problems & Solutions in Small Business Management: Case Studies from Small Business Forum (1995); ISBN: 0936894717
Maxwell Sroge, United States Mail Order Industry (2nd ed. 1994); ISBN: 0844234516
Start Your Own Business: 101 Extra Income Ideas (1996); ISBN: 0136032672
Start Your Own Catering Business (1996); ISBN: 0136033091
Start Your Own Childcare Business (1996); ISBN: 0136033253
Start Your Own Coffee & Tea Store (1996); ISBN: 0136032753
Start Your Own Desktop Publishing Business (1996); ISBN: 0136032834
Start Your Own Gift Basket Business (1996); ISBN: 0136032915
Start Your Own Import/Export Business (1996); ISBN: 0136030289
Start Your Own Information Broker Service (1997); ISBN: 0136033172
Start Your Own Mail Order Business (1996); ISBN: 0136030513

Start Your Own Money-Making Computer Business (1996); ISBN: 0136032265

Start Your Own Newsletter Publishing Business (1996); ISBN: 0136033334

Start Your Own Resume Writing Business (1996); ISBN: 0136032346

Start Your Own Secretarial Service Business (1996); ISBN: 0136032427

Start Your Own Temporary Help Agency (1996); ISBN: 0136032591

William Sullivan, Human Resource for Small Businesses (1996); ISBN: 0471149470

Harvey Summers, Operating a Desktop Video Service on Your Home-Based PC (1994); ISBN: 007064545X

Don Taylor & Jeanne Smalling Archer, Up Against the WalMarts: How Your Business Can Prosper in the Shadow of the Retail Giants (1996); ISBN: 0814479162

Lawrence W. Tuller, The Small Business Valuation Book (1998); ISBN: 1580620051

Herb D. Vest & Lynn R. Niedermeier, Wealth: How to Get It and How to Keep It (1995); ISBN: 0814478913

H. Skip Weitzen & Rick Parkhill, Infopreneurs: Online & Global (1996); ISBN: 0471140244

Jane Wesman, Dive Right in the Sharks Won't Bite: Entrepreneurial Woman's Guide to Success (reprint ed. 1997); ISBN: 0137372302

Cheryl Woodard, Starting & Running a Successful Newsletter or Magazine (3rd ed. 2002); ISBN 0-87337-8474

R. Woodson, Paper Shield: Avoiding Confusion, Conflicts & Lawsuits (1996); ISBN: 1568420536

F. Selected Federal Laws Relevant to Microenterprise Development

Program for Investment in Microentrepreneurs (PRIME)
15 U.S.C. § 634 (b)(6), Pub. L. No. 106-102.

PRIME authorizes the U.S. Small Business Administration to make grants to "qualified organizations" to provide technical assistance and training for disadvantaged entrepreneurs. The aim is to build the organizational capacity of MED organizations to provide technical assistance and training, fund research and development of "best practices" in microenterprise development.

New Markets Tax Credit (NMTC) Program
H12392, Dec. 15, 2000, Sec. 45 D.

The NMTC Program, administered by the Community Development Financial Institution (CDFI) Fund of the U.S. Department of Treasury, was enacted by Congress in December 2000 as part of the Community Renewal Tax Relief Act of 2000. It is a complex tax credit program modeled, in part, on the Low Income Housing Tax Credit Program. Designed over seven years, it allocates $15 billion in tax credit investment authority, which generates credits equal to 39% of an investment. Investors receive tax credits and an opportunity to profit from their investment in exchange for equity investments in a Community Development Entity (CDE). CDEs must demonstrate that their primary mission is to serve the needs of low-income communities through investment capital in equity or loans and accountability to low-income community residents through representation on the CDE's governing or advisory board. The program is new and its application to MED is untested, however, several NMTC recipients have indicated an interest in supporting microbusiness development.

The Community Development Block Grant Program (CDBG)
Housing and Community Development Act of 1974, §101(c); 42 U.S.C. § 5301(c).

The CDBG program is the largest single source of funds available for urban economic development. Under the entitlement program and the state administered program, communities receive CDBG funds based on need. Entitlement communities—metropolitan cities and urban counties—receive the largest proportion. Local governments determine how to spend funds.

Several general categories define how recipients must use CDBG funds: acquisition and development of real property; slum clearance activities; public services; relocation assistance; rehabilitation and preservation of housing; economic development; and urban planning and design. Within this framework, recipients can choose among twenty-four specific activities, five of which address economic development. These include: acquisition, construction, reconstruction, rehabilitation or installation of commercial and industrial buildings, public facilities, structures, site improvement and other real property and equipment; loans and other assistance for for-profit development projects; the provision of services for economic development projects; and assistance to microenterprises. See § 105(a), (14), (15), (17), (23); 42 U.S.C. § 5305(a)(14), (15), (17), (23). The use of all funds must, however, meet several sets of rules. The 1992 Amendments to the Housing and Community Development Act, Hous. and Comm. Dev. Act. of 1992, Pub. L. No. 102-550, § 807(c)(3), Oct. 28, 1992, give special priority to microenterprises, specifying that recipients should reserve one percent of their CDBG grant each year for assistance to microenterprises. Similarly, the 1995 Amendments to the Housing and Community Development Act, 42 U.S.C.A. § 5302(a) (1995), allow the CDBG program to be a major contributor to providing jobs for low-income persons and assistance for microenterprises.

The Job Opportunities for Low-Income Individuals Program (JOLI) Social Security Act, Title XI, § 1110, as amended, Pub. L. Nos. 86778, 88452, 90265, 99190, and 100485, as amended, 42 U.S.C. § 1310.

This program, part of the Office of Community Services of the Department of Health and Human Services, provides grants to private nonprofit organizations to determine and illustrate ways to facilitate new jobs and business opportunities for welfare recipients and other low-income individuals at or below poverty level. JOLI supports programs for microenterprise training, technical assistance and credit, as well as other strategies to support new business creation, business expansion, and access to non-traditional jobs for minorities and women. Acknowledging the success of the JOLI program, the most recent welfare reform legislation dropped the program's demonstration status and increased the funds it receives from $6.5 million to $25 million. This will permit nonprofits in the United States to create countless new businesses and new jobs for welfare recipients and other low-income people.

The Microloan Program
Small Business Act § 7 (m), 15, U.S.C. § 636 (m) (1994), *as amended by* Pub. L. No. 105-135, § 201(c)(1), 111 Stat. 2592 (1997).

Implemented in 1992 as a demonstration project, this program of the Small Business Administration is designed to make loans through intermediaries to very small businesses in poor communities. It also offers grant monies to qualifying entities that offer technical assistance in areas such as marketing and management. The Small Business Credit and Opportunity Enhancement Act of 1992 expanded the Microloan program by enabling the Small Business Administration to issue funds to more intermediaries. This program was made permanent in 1997.

Financial Institutions Reform Recovery and Enforcement Act (FIRREA)
Pub. L. No. 101-73, §721, 103 Stat. 183, 423; 12 U.S.C. § 1430(i)(1989).

FIRREA directed the Federal Home Loan Banks (FHLBank) to create a program to provide funding to financial institution members of the FHLBank System for community oriented mortgage lending. The Community Investment Program (CIP) provides discounted advances (loans) to FHLBank members that lend the funds to their customers for commercial and economic development activities that either benefit low and moderate income households by providing employment or services or are located in low and moderate income neighborhoods. Microenterprise programs have borrowed some of these funds.

The Community Reinvestment Act of 1977 (CRA)
12 U.S.C. §§ 2901–07 (1994).

CRA requires the federal bank regulatory agencies to encourage banks to meet the credit needs of low- and moderate-income people. This is accomplished by assessing a bank's lending record and taking that record into account when considering a bank's application to expand. Community residents can challenge a bank's application to expand on the grounds that it has failed to meet community needs. The bank's application can also be denied because it has an inadequate CRA record. New CRA regulations implement four performance tests, one of which requires banks to disclose information about their small business and community development loans. In response to community reinvestment activists who wanted more information about lending practices, Congress passed amendments to the Financial Institutions Reform, Recovery, and Enforcement Act of 1989 (FIRREA). These require federal regulators who evaluate lender compliance to share their evaluations with the institutions evaluated and to disclose their findings to the public. FIRREA also modified the Home Mortgage Disclosure Act by requiring lenders to document the numbers and dollar amounts of loan applications received, approved, or rejected, by race, gender, and income level of applicants. The Home Mortgage Disclosure Act of 1975 (HMDA), 12 U.S.C. §§ 2801–11 (1994), requires lenders with assets of $20 million or more to report the number and dollar value of mortgages that they originate or purchase every year. Residents can uses this information to identify the lenders that reinvest in their community and those who do not.

Revenue Reconciliation Act of 1993 (OBRA)
Title XIII of the Omnibus Budget Reconciliation Act of 1993, Pub. L. No. 103-66, §§ 13301–03, 107 Stat. 312, 543; 26 U.S.C. §§ 1391–94, 1396, 1397 (1994).

This Act made available one million dollars for each Empowerment Zone and Enterprise Community (EZEC). One hundred million dollars in grants are available for each urban empowerment zone, forty million for each rural empowerment zone, and approximately three million for each enterprise community. The Empowerment Zones are Atlanta, Chicago, Baltimore, Detroit, Harlem/Washington Heights/South Bronx, NY, and Philadelphia, PA/Camden, NJ. There are over 60 Enterprise Communities; for a complete list and other information see www.hud.gov/cpd/ezec/ezbyez.html.

The grant funds are to be used to implement three broad goals: economic self-support to prevent, reduce, or eliminate dependency; self-sufficiency, including reducing or preventing dependency; and preventing or remedying neglect, abuse, or exploitation of children and adults unable to protect their own interests. Employment training, entrepreneurism, development of microenterprise loan funds, self-employment training and enhanced transportation services to improve access of zone residents to high growth job areas outside of the zone are several examples of the appropriate use of these funds.

G. Recent Literature on Socially Responsible Investing

Domini, Amy. Socially Responsible Investing: Making a Difference and Making Money; Dearborn Trade Publishing; 1st ed. (January 15, 2001).

Brill, Hal, Jack A. Brill & Cliff Feigenbaum. Investing with Your Values (Conscientious Commerce); New Society Pub; Reprint ed. (October 1, 2000).

Fehrenbacher, Scott. Put Your Money Where Your Morals Are: A Guide to Values-Based Investing; Broadman & Holman Publishers (October 2001).

Sparkes, Russell. Socially Responsible Investment: A Global Revolution; John Wiley & Sons (December 6, 2002).

Glickman, Marshall. The Mindful Money Guide: Creating Harmony Between Your Values and Your Finances; Ballantine Books (May 18, 1999).

Connections, Newsletter of the Co-op America Business Network and Social Investment Forum, www.coopamerica.org/cabn/connections/index.html.

Social Investment Forum, 2001 Report on Socially Responsible Investing Trends in the United States, www.socialinvest.org/area/research/trends/2001-Trends.htm.

Booth, Tamzin. "Ethics Lesson: Principles Pay—Socially Responsible Investing Can Also Be a 'Good' Way to Make a Profit"; The Wall Street Journal Europe, June 20, 2000, at 31.

Price, Margaret. "In Good Conscience: Refined Niche Funds Focus on Targeted Social Values"; Newsday, March 11, 2001, at F6.

Hutton, R. Bruce et al. "Socially Responsible Investing: Growing Issues and New Opportunities"; 37 Bus. & Soc. 281 (1998).

Kurtz, Lloyd. "Investment in Minority-Owned Media: A Social Investor's Perspective"; 51 Federal Communications Law Journal, May 1999 at 681.